The Portuguese Military
and the State

D1608192

The Portuguese Military and the State

Rethinking Transitions in Europe and Latin America

Lawrence S. Graham

Westview Press

BOULDER • SAN FRANCISCO • OXFORD

Copyright © 1993 by Westview Press, Inc.

Published in 1993 in the United States of America by Westview Press, Inc., 5500 Central Avenue, Boulder, Colorado 80301-2877, and in the United Kingdom by Westview Press, 36 Lonsdale Road, Summertown, Oxford OX2 7EW

Library of Congress Cataloging-in-Publication Data
Graham, Lawrence S.
    The Portuguese military and the state : rethinking transitions in Europe and Latin America / by Lawrence S. Graham.
        p. cm.
    Includes bibliographical references and index.
    ISBN 0-8133-8613-6
    1. Civil-military relations—Portugal. 2. Portugal—Politics and government—1974– I. Title.
JN8515.G73 1993
322'.5'09469—dc20
                                                    93-25302
                                                    CIP

Printed and bound in the United States of America

The paper used in this publication meets the requirements
of the American National Standard for Permanence of Paper
for Printed Library Materials Z39.48-1984.

10   9   8   7   6   5   4   3   2   1

For our Sintra friends from times long past

The Croft de Mouras

Jim and Peggy Jeffries

Phyllis Milne

Contents

Preface

Since one of the objectives in writing this book has been to bring into focus 20 years of research on Portugal—published in a variety of articles, chapters, and edited books—it is appropriate to begin by acknowledging the fact that this research has been greatly facilitated by contact, discussion, and debate with other scholars in Portugal and in the United States. While there are many, many people with whom I have interacted over the years in going to and from Portugal, my understanding and love for things Portuguese is due first of all to colleagues in Portugal. Among them specific mention should be made of Mário Bacalhau, Manuel Braga da Cruz, António Barreto, Manuel Villaverde Cabral, Manuel de Lucena, António Costa Pinto, and José Blanco. In the United States four individuals stand out: Miguel Bensaude, Thomas Bruneau, Stanley Payne, and Douglas Wheeler. I also would like to thank Suzanne Colwell, Department of Government, at The University of Texas at Austin for her help with preparing this project for publication.

However, in acknowledging the gratitude I owe these people for support, especially at times when it has been difficult professionally to sustain an interest in Portugal within the United States, none of the ideas or interpretations included herein should be attributed to them. The interpretations made and the conclusions reached are entirely my own. I have endeavored to be succinct in my interpretation of Portuguese affairs to see if I might elicit the interest of others, busy with their own pursuits and agendas, so that they might pause for a moment and consider what has been going on in contemporary Portugal.

The years entailed in getting from 1971, when I first travelled to Portugal, to 1992 coincide with events in Portugal which provide insight into and an understanding of a broader world in transition during the 1970s and the 1980s and which transcend the experience of any one particular national community. While a great deal has been written on

the transitions from authoritarian to democratic rule, first in Southern
Europe, later in South America, and more recently in Eastern Europe,
Portugal's transition has received much less attention, except for a
monographic literature that speaks to the uniqueness of the Portuguese
case. However, as the scope of these transitions has broadened to
embrace not just politics but economics as well, the Portuguese case has
become more relevant in that its problems with political, economic, and
social change are more akin to those encountered in the transitions in the
Balkans than those that have taken place elsewhere in Southern Europe
or South America.

This perspective, when applied to the Portuguese-speaking world at
large, has led me to conclude that now more so than ever there is a place
for work in the social sciences that is Luso-Brazilian in focus. In studies
of language and culture such a perspective is an old one and has
continued to produce a literature that spans Europe, South America, and
Africa. But in the study of politics, the state, and society this perspective
has never been considered relevant, except perhaps in its appropriation
by the *ultras* (right-wing nationalists) to shore up a collapsing imperial
state in the late 1960s and early 1970s and to justify Portuguese
colonialism in Africa. Yet, as a consequence of having re-entered
Lusophone Africa (through applied work on the Angolan and
Mozambican transitions from 1989 through 1992) and more recently
having returned to Brazil after eight years (to evaluate applied work on
citizenship, social movements, and labor organizations outside the state),
I have become convinced that there is much to be gained by comparing
and contrasting the "triangulation" of institutions and cultures linking
together Portugal, the African countries of Angola and Mozambique, and
Brazil.

The point of departure in this case is Portugal since its 1974
revolution. The underlying paradigm is centered in a re-examination of
Raymundo Faoro's classic *Os Donos do Poder: Formação do Patronato Político
Brasileiro*.[1] In the upheavals that have swept across the Luso-Brazilian
world since the 1970s, there are sufficient parallels in the articulation
between state, civil society, and the military in these four transitions
(Portugal, Brazil, Angola, and Mozambique) to warrant special attention.
But the problem is that the kind of state that has emerged—sometimes
strong and more often weak—cannot be understood as a framework for
socializing governing elites into particular patterns of behavior and

perceptions of the political world without looking first at the military institution and the relationships that have evolved between the state, civil society, and the military over time.

In the evolution of the state in the Luso-Brazilian world, the interaction between civilian and military bureaucrats has been continuous enough so that civilian and military bureaucracy are in a real sense inseparable insofar as bureaucratic roles are to be viewed within the framework created by the state, or what I will frequently call throughout this book "the state apparatus." During the monarchical era this could be seen in the attachment of what were called "civilian and military households" to the royal household. Today both in Brazil and Portugal this practice continues in the Office of the Presidency of the Republic in what are called in Portuguese *a casa civil* and *a casa militar*. It is only now that the official ideology of state socialism, adapted and applied to Angola and Mozambique at independence, is being stripped away that it is becoming possible to reenter the bureaucratized world of government there, to understand these parallels in the conceptualization of the relationship between state and society, coupled with the severe constraints placed on state power in those transitions as a consequence of prolonged conflict.

Before these larger parallels can be addressed and the theme of maintaining the integrity of national territory in the face of considerable diversity can be engaged, it becomes essential first to block in the particulars of the Portuguese case, since it is there that this type of state has its origins—before one interjects the very different experiences of each of these other societies in equally different parts of the world. At the center of this conceptualization lies the problem of how to analyze a state that is weak institutionally but quite successful in its ability to transmit cultural values that emphasize maintaining a sense of national community in the face of adversity. There are, for example, enormous differences among Portugal, Brazil, and Mozambique. These differences have led scholars—particularly those in the United States writing within the established traditions of European, Latin American, and African studies—to use a geographic point of reference and to overlook what I would call the distinctiveness of the world the Portuguese created through their overseas expansion. Yet in all three transitions—albeit with each at very different points in confronting state building, nation building, and modernization pressures—a framework for governance has evolved that has had the capacity to emphasize the values of survival through its ability to socialize governing elites into ways of thinking and acting that lead to the definition and maintenance of a national community, despite circumstances to the contrary. Within each of these transitions, current elites (those who hold power) are engaged once again in the reformulation of state apparatuses (through which one can govern today) and in the redefinition of national communities (with the capacity to reduce the divisiveness of localism) in the latter part of the twentieth century.

Nevertheless, it is important to emphasize that these patterns do not necessarily speak to cultural uniqueness but rather to structural choices linked to how elites in weak states seek to define and maintain national communities in what is often a hostile environment for their survival. The cases I would use to challenge arguments linked to Portuguese exceptionalism are those of Romania and Serbia.[2]

The first step in developing this argument involves analyzing the Portuguese case in such a way that it becomes theoretically relevant. To do so involves understanding that the reconstitution of civil society and the emergence of civilian leaders with democratic values alone are insufficient to sustain a democratic regime in these cases. Into this situation one must interject consideration both of the military (as an independent actor, national institution, and catalyst for change) and the state (as an apparatus composed of distinct civilian and military bureaucracies), to understand what is necessary in these instances to move to the consolidation of a new regime compatible with new ways of thinking about governance in the 1990s. The difficulty encountered here, in working with contemporary Portugal, has been how to bridge the gap between studies of the military and studies of the state (defined exclusively in terms of civilians), in the presence of a social science literature that speaks only to civilian actors outside state constructs once a democratic transition is underway.

Lawrence S. Graham
Austin, Texas

Notes

1. Raymundo Faoro, *Os Donos do Poder: Formação do Patronato Político Brasileiro* (Porto Alegre: Editora Globo, 1975 [2nd revised edition, 2 vols.]). Faoro's thesis centers around the bureaucratic structures identified with the development of the Portuguese state historically, their transfer to Brazil, and their acculturation to the Brazilian environment. The key point in his argument, as utilized here, centers around the concept *o estamento burocrático* (the bureaucratic strata of society), with its emphasis on the centrality of the state and the socialization of elites into patterns of political behavior linked to the values of centralism, cultural cohesiveness (despite social, ethnic, and geographic diversity), and patrimonialism. For a summary statement of his argument in the context of monarchical Brazil, see vol. 1, pp. 387-94. In utilizing this concept here, however, it is important to emphasize that I have adapted it and revised it to focus on the cultural dimensions of bureaucracy and the interplay in the Luso-Brazilian world between state and society.

2. The most cogent statement of these perspectives that I have seen, in a way that speaks to Romania's current transition is: István Deák, "Survivors," *The New York Review of Books*, 5 March 1992, pp. 43-51. Nevertheless, here as elsewhere in current studies of Romania, little attention is given to the state apparatus as a cultural phenomenon, integrated with the definition and maintenance of a national community. An even more fascinating case in this interpenetration of state and society with the survival of a distinct national community in what I would call a hostile setting is that of Serbia. But there one has to be able to link together three institutions and the way in which they interact with the state apparatus: the military, civilian authorities, and the Serbian Orthodox Church. For a statement of this latter perspective, the differentiation among different variants of nationalism, and the use of the construct of traumatic nationalism to understand Serbia's current aggressive behavior, see Sabrina Petra Ramet, "The Serbian Church and the Serbian Nation," paper presented at the panel on "Religion in Eastern Europe in the Post-Communist Era," 1992 National Convention of the American Association for the Advancement of Slavic Studies (Phoenix, Arizona: 19-22 November 1992).

1

Rethinking the Breakdown of Authoritarian Regimes in Southern Europe, Latin America, and Eastern Europe

The breakdown of authoritarian regimes and the transition to more open forms of governance and new market structures entail enormous changes. This is especially the case in the context of disintegrating political, social, and and economic systems identified with the old order. In transitions of this type, when there is the absence of a coherent civilian-based opposition movement with organized mass support and leadership cohesion, replacement of the previous governing elite with the partisans of change and control of the state apparatus are not easily accomplished. In these settings, the military is likely to become a key player in determining political outcomes. Such was the experience of Portugal during its transition from authoritarian to democratic politics.

This pattern of politics, present for so long in the political history of Southern Europe and South America, has largely been overlooked in the theories and accounts of the transitions to democracy in the 1980s. There are several reasons for this. First, in those countries, with the exception of Portugal and Turkey, by the mid-1970s the military had lost much of its credibility as an institution capable of resolving civil conflict because of its involvement in the authoritarian regimes under attack. While the extent of military involvement in questions of governance varied greatly, from the extreme of military dominance of virtually all aspects of the governmental process in Greece and Argentina to an increasingly marginal role for the nation's armed forces in Spain at the end of the Franco regime, in all these cases there was the desire within the military institution to disengage from politics and to depoliticize the armed forces. Second, in each of these cases strong civilian opposition movements had arisen, with new leaders capable of mobilizing mass support in favor of democracy and civilian rule and constituting alternative governments.

In the second wave of transitions—those in the Soviet Union and Eastern Europe which began at the end of the 1980s—the situation has become much more complex. There the necessity of radical economic change has accompanied desire for a brusk change in politics. The consequence of the convergence of radical political and economic reforms has been great uncertainty within these new governments. How to establish a new course of action and to implement economic and social policies necessary to open up society but contrary to popular wishes and expectations has entailed painful and cruel choices. In cases like Poland, the Czech and Slovak Republics, and Hungary, civilian opposition movements and their leaders stood ready to assume control of the instruments of government once the Soviet Union ceased to guarantee the Communist regimes in power. Hence, there it has been possible to focus attention on economic reform and a lively debate has ensued over the appropriate economic models and implementation strategies to be followed. Certainly, conflict and protest have ensued, but they have been insufficient to threaten the legitimacy of these new regimes. However, in the Balkans not only did the Communist old guard demonstrate a capacity to survive the upheavals and to reconstitute itself as a potent political force but also, due to their ties with the military and security forces (internal as well as external), the military has emerged as a major stakeholder with decided institutional interests of its own in influencing the outcomes. As a consequence, in Southeastern Europe the break with the old regime has been neither as clear-cut nor as easy to make in separating civilian and military groups vying for power from prior existing interests and commitments to established concepts of state and nation. In this setting, autonomous state apparatuses have disappeared and prior assumptions regarding the capacity of these governments to act independently of the political and social forces in the societies under their jurisdiction have dissolved.

If these observations are kept in mind, there are two major components in assessing outcomes in transitions that current case material overlooks or minimizes: civil-military relations and the state. The interaction between these two variables—the role of the military and the capacity of the state to instigate policy change constitute major components in the transitions underway since 1989. They were also present earlier in the Portuguese transition. Because they are central to understanding how that country achieved a consolidated democracy by the beginnings of the 1990s, it is especially appropriate in the present context to reassess the Portuguese transition to see if we can understand more clearly what the choices are and what must take place in the movement toward democratic governance and competitive markets in badly divided societies, where the legacy of the past hangs like a shroud over the present. Yet neither the military nor the state has received the attention it deserves in the existing transitions literature, be it generic or case specific. In this setting Portugal's experience extending from 1974 to 1989 takes on particular meaning as a first step in explaining success and failure more effectively in societies where democratic outcomes are achieved by intent and design, despite enormous obstacles.

Civil-military relations constitute a crucial element in assessing outcomes in all transitions from authoritarian rule. In reassessing these transitions in Brazil and the Southern Cone, Alfred Stepan has clearly pointed out that in those cases the military institution remained a major player and actively participated in the accords and the accomodations worked out.[1] Whether or not democratic rule can be expected to survive is linked very closely to actions within this domain. Yet, to date, little effort has been made to tie this dimension of politics to the emergence of civilian political movements and parties and how civilian and military authorities must work out a new set of accomodations once the assumptions under which they have operated in the prior regime have disappeared. Since a consolidated democratic regime cannot be achieved without commitment from the military that it will not intervene in politics regardless of electoral outcomes and that it will ignore civilian appeals to the military for assistance on their behalf, how acceptance of civilian oversight authority is achieved takes on great significance.

The second component in these transitions warranting special consideration is the institutional setting provided by the state.[2] The issue here concerns the ability of political leaders, once they constitute a new regime, to implement policies of central importance to successor governments, in this case democracies. Experience to date with this issue suggests that three policy arenas take on particular importance in determining the ability of new governments to meet the demands placed upon them: (1) civil-military relations, (2) economic policy, and (3) social policy.[3] In current discussions, questions of economic restructuring—in such areas as the development of competitive market economies, privatization, structural adjustment and policy reform—have dominated the policy agenda.[4] But this debate has been structured largely in technical terms according to the conditions necessary to make markets work. Yet, effective action in each of these areas involves interaction with a variety of groups in society, each of whom has its own particular agenda and viewpoints on how scarce resources are to be allocated. Thus, it should not surprise anyone that the process of implementing policy in each of these three arenas becomes intensely political for the simple reason that, in the context of limited economic resources, everyone has a stake in the outcomes because everyone stands to gain or lose from the actions taken.

Up until this point (1992), however, the literature on transitions has been dominated by concern with those cases where pacts and carefully negotiated agreements have assured relatively peaceful transitions to democratic rule. By focusing attention on the interaction among these political leaders, the assumption has been that this is essentially a process driven by civilian elites. Agreements reached by these new political actors, in turn, are seen as facilitating the assumption of control of the state apparatus by duly elected civilian authorities. While this has been the pattern in Spain and in Chile, this is not true everywhere.

In countries like Portugal and the former Yugoslavia, when transitions become tied in with the redefinition of the political community that is to be governed by the state and mass political movements develop independently of leadership preferences, the policy dilemmas to be confronted are far greater and the prospects for political turmoil, much more likely. Such is the experience of states in the midst of transition in Southeastern Europe as well as within the former Union of Soviet Socialist Republics. Likewise, while the military has been relatively quiescent in South American politics, in the continent's Andean regions—especially Peru—yet another upheaval is going on, as state and nation there too are being redefined.

In these settings, one cannot conclude that we have seen the last of the military in politics. The same applies to evaluation of the military in Brazil and the Southern Cone. While there is no doubt about the fact that the military in each of these instances identified its own institutional self-interest with support for democracy once these transitions began, in each instance the military has retained decisive veto authority. This is the clearest in the case of Chile, but even in Argentina where the military was thoroughly discredited by its involvement in the internal "Dirty War" against its own civilian population and its loss of the external war over the Falklands/Malvinas to Great Britain, it cannot be assumed that the military will stay out of politics if and when the civilian forces with which they are not in accord assume power and control of the state or existing governments move in directions contrary to what they define as their institutional interests.[5]

In such a context there is much to be learned by returning to the Portuguese case. For in comparative perspective, now that Portugal has achieved the status of a consolidated democracy, it becomes very clear that the Portuguese transition to democracy was an exception to the pattern set in Southern Europe during the 1970s, most specifically that established by Spain. But, in the world of the 1990s where political and economic uncertainties abound in the Balkans, in areas comprising the former U.S.S.R., and in major portions of South America, the Portuguese case has greater relevance. For, like these republics, Portugal during the early 1970s was a fragmented society in which issues regarding prior definitions of state and nation rose to the forefront and the previous basis for defining national unity was called into question. While there are elements of the unique in each of these cases—viz, Portugal's overseas territories which gained independence in 1975—Portuguese experience is of relevance in understanding the political, social, and economic dynamics of those societies where societal divisions are so great that transitions from authoritarian rule call into question prior definitions of state, society, and national economy.

In cases characterized by social upheaval, the military is almost certain to emerge as a key institution and exercise its option to act unilaterally. As ruling civilian coalitions dissolve and new actors in leadership positions fail to coalesce in their attempt to reshape the old regime and the economy, the military's original mission to defend the nation can easily become the rationale for direct intervention. This is because the military constitutes a stakeholder with vested interests in determining policy outcomes by virtue of its concern with national security issues and the integrity of state and nation.

Yet, as past experience has shown, once the military as institution participates actively in policy debates and involves itself in questions of governance, the very fragmentation present in civil society permeates the military institution, disrupting its internal coherency and its capacity to function either as government or as an effective unitary force for maintaining civil order. This is the pattern that emerged early on in the Portuguese revolution, in 1974. It also has been present in Yugoslavia in 1991 where, as the military sought to arrest the move toward independence in Slovenia and Croatia, its own integrity as a federal institution was called into question by the absence of a clear-cut foreign threat and the divisiveness of internal politics. These internal divisions led not to the removal of the military from participation in questions of policy but to its redefinition as a fighting force once it perceived its own institutional interests to be endangered. Thus, while at this time (February 1993) it is impossible to predict the outcomes of the current conflict involving the new Yugoslav state, composed of Serbia and Montenegro, the military remains a distinct actor.

While the dynamics involving civilians and the military within the former Yugoslav federation are vastly different from the bureaucratic empire in place in Portugal in 1974, the initial results have been quite similar: rapid disintegration of the capacity of the central government to control areas under its jurisdiction—prior to the initiation of the transition—and enormous debates within the military institution as its prior image as a monolithic institution designed to meet a common external threat collapses. As military factionalism increases, survival of the military as a coherent institution becomes linked to its willingness to share power with civilian allies. At this juncture how power is distributed among military and civilian authorities constitutes a fundamental factor influencing the formation of the successor regime and determining whether or not a democratic transition can continue.

While there are instances of successful transitions to democracy since World War II, in which the military was sidelined from the beginning (viz, the cases of Italy in 1945, Costa Rica in 1948, Greece in 1974, and Spain in 1976), these are the exception rather than the rule. Elsewhere, much more common is the pattern in which the military becomes actively engaged in negotiating the terms of the transition with civilian leaders and must agree to the conditions under which the latter will hold power before it retreats to the sidelines. From the wings, with its institutional identity intact, military officers in such cases can continue to monitor and pressure the new governments informally if they see them moving in directions with which they are not in accord (viz, the cases of Brazil, Chile, and Uruguay). Yet, most current theories of transition and individual country case studies of the return to civilian rule assume that there is an inevitability to civilian rule once mass-based, coherent political parties emerge.

Reexamination of this issue in broader, comparative context in Europe and Latin America suggests a pattern of politics much less pronounced in the transitions characteristic of the 1970s and 1980s. But it has become of transcendental importance in weighing the prospects for successful democratic transition and consolidation, against breakdown and the return of authoritarian rule, during the 1990s. Seen from this vantage point, the presence of the military as a stakeholder and how its leadership is to be convinced of its need to support civilian governance in the restructuring of power relationships constitutes a significant prior condition influencing subsequent political outcomes.

In seeking to span the gap between the civil-military relations literature (viz, the work of Alfred Stepan and discussions of the Brazilian transition centered in the analysis of the military) and the "transitions" literature on Southern Europe and Latin America (as best exemplified by the work of Guillermo O'Donnell, Philippe Schmitter, and Laurence Whitehead), this case study of the Portuguese transition and consolidation of a democratic regime seeks to clarify a particular set of issues.[6] In transitions without successful consolidation early on, what are the conditions that later lead to the institutionalization of a democratic regime? Although much more attention was devoted to the Spanish case as a prototype during the 1980s, the argument developed here is that Portuguese experience is far more relevant than previously thought in assessing current political outcomes in Latin America and Eastern Europe.[7] It is especially relevant in seeking to understand more fully the options present in reshaping political, economic, and social institutions cross-nationally as a new generation of political leaders takes power in Central Europe, the Balkans, Iberia, and South America during the 1990s.

These concerns lie at the core of this interest in reexamining the Portuguese case. But, in writing this book, the goal has not been simply to add another volume to the literature that has emerged on Portugal as an individual country case. Rather, my interest centers in the implications of the Portuguese case for understanding more fully broader, cross-national patterns in politics and governance in which we must reconceptualize and rethink the role of the state. At the same time, in order to block in the Portuguese case and to establish its relevance to the issues raised here, what becomes necessary is to establish first what occurred in Portugal that supports these perspectives and concerns. It is to that topic then—the particularities of the Portuguese case—that we must first turn our attention.

Notes

1. Alfred Stepan, *Rethinking Military Politics: Brazil and the Southern Cone* (Princeton, NJ: Princeton University Press, 1988).

2. These considerations are based on what I consider to be a seminal work in rethinking the role of the state in society: Peter Evans, Dietrich Rueschemeyer, and Theda Skocpol (eds.), *Bringing the State Back In* (Princeton, NJ: Princeton University Press, 1985).

3. These are the conclusions reached in a workshop on "Democratic Transitions in Eastern Europe and Latin America," sponsored by the Center for Soviet and East European Studies, University of Texas at Austin, April 8-9, 1991. In this meeting participating scholars reviewed the existing literature, prepared working papers on various related topics, and discussed at length the major issues to be confronted. Additional relevant papers and prior discussions dealing with these topics are to be found in the proceedings of two international meetings: "Contemporary Societies in Comparative Perspective: Eastern Europe and Latin America in the Twentieth Century," Pultusk and Warsaw, Poland (May 28 - June 2, 1990), organized by the East European Research Group, and the international colloquium co-sponsored by FLACSO and the Universidad de Guadalajara, "Transitions to Democracy in Europe and Latin America," Guadalajara, Mexico (January 21-25, 1991). Papers from the latter are to be found in C.B. Solano, J.L. Barros Horcasitas, J. Hurtado (eds.), *Transiciones a la Democracia en Europa y América Latina* (Mexico: Facultad Latinoamericana de Ciencias Sociales y Universidad de Guadalajara, 1991).

4. For a recent summary of these issues and the political controversy they engender, see Joan M. Nelson (ed.), *Economic Crisis and Policy Choice: The Politics of Adjustment in the Third World* (Princeton, NJ: Princeton University Press, 1990).

5. The scholar who has done the most to define the specifics entailed in establishing civilian oversight authority and the circumstances under which the military retain the capacity for independent action is Jorge Zaverucha. See two recent papers by him: "Degree of Military Political Autonomy During the Spanish, Argentine, and Brazilian Transitions," LASA XVII International Congress (Los Angeles, CA: September 24-27, 1992) and "The 1988 Brazilian Constitution or How to Harm Civilian Control over the Military," in Lawrence S. Graham (ed.), "Political and Economic Transitions in Eastern Europe and Latin America" (unpublished book manuscript).

6. Stepan, *Rethinking Military Politics*, and Guillermo O'Donnell, Philippe C. Schmitter, and Laurence Whitehead (eds.), *Transitions from Authoritarian Rule: Prospects for Democracy* (Baltimore, MD: The Johns Hopkins University Press, 1986).

7. The most recent statement of this concern and its re-examination from a critical perspective is to be found in Kenneth Maxwell, "Spain's Transition to Democracy: A Model for Eastern Europe?" in Nils H. Wessell (ed.), *The New Europe: Revolution in East-West Relations* (New York: The Academy of Political Science, 1991).

2

The Military's Role in the Transition to a Democratic Portugal

In Portugal's long history as an independent polity—in what is probably the world's oldest nation-state—the decade of the 1970s will surely stand out as one of its most momentous. During that period the country passed from the apogee of imperial illusion, as a bureaucratic-authoritarian regime with multicontinental dimensions in Africa and Asia, to the brink of revolutionary conflict and upheaval, and from there into a small, stable Western European democratic regime confined to the Iberian peninsula and two Atlantic island groups. Just as political forces reached the point where further confrontation would have made bloodshed and prolonged social conflict unavoidable, a majority in the body politic drew back to a position, supported by a small but influential group of officers, where they opted for resolving further differences at the ballot box. From there, as the new military leadership consciously depoliticized the military institution, politics evolved from unstable, fragile party alignments centered around individual civilian and military personalities, into a new set of arrangements characterized by democratic pluralism.

As the decade ended, Portugal found itself governed by a semi-presidential parliamentary system. With a coalition of center and conservative forces dominant, the extremes in Portuguese politics since have been checked. The left opposition has been willing to abide by majority decision as long as its recourse to electoral competition and its use of the strike to redress grievances is not placed in jeopardy, while the old authoritarian right has simply disappeared as a consequence of age and the inability of younger leaders to establish a large enough constituency to have an impact on the nation's politics. This experience has collapsed into a single decade political developments that elsewhere have a far longer history. To understand why this is the case one must consider the military as an essential ingredient in the Portuguese transition.

The Problem

Despite the importance of the military in Portugal's transition to democracy, substantive research on civil-military relations during these years is not easily located. The topic remains a Pandora's box that most people in Portugal would like to considered closed, for it is filled with the conflicting ideologies, conceptual rigidities, and intellectual and popular biases that were so openly manifested during the mid-1970s. This is because the military was intimately tied up with the conflict and the redefinition of Portuguese politics that was underway in the broader society during these years. A key component of the strategy to depoliticize the military was to take it entirely out of public affairs and to remove its officers from further involvement in questions of political controversy.

Just as the "transitions" literature in comparative politics cannot find an easy way to account for how a stable democratic polity emerged in Portugal, so too one can search far and wide for a discussion of the role of the military in this process without success. Yet just a few years before, be it in the popular press or learned discussions of politics in revolutionary Portugal, the MFA—the Armed Forces Movement with its radical officers—was centerplace.

The same observation can be made about the wider body of cross-national literature on the military in politics, much of which is based on Latin American experience. For example, neither the literature on the South American military—with its emphasis on what was known as the "new professionalism" in the 1970s and how it led to new military involvement in politics—nor that written by generalists eschewing area perspectives—with its emphasis on political party institutionalization and stable legislative roles—is sufficient to deal with the subtilties of the Portuguese case.

To account for Portuguese experience one must use an interactive institutional model within which both the military and the state are dealt with organizationally as well as according to the behavior of individual military and civilian actors. This entails conceptualizing the military institution as a large amorphous bureaucracy with a key group of actors, in constant contact with other actors in the institution's political, social, and economic environment. To date no one has taken a bureaucratic perspective on the Portuguese military seriously, yet I would argue that it is impossible to identify sustained military roles across the 1970s and into the 1980s without relating them to the organizational dimension. Once military officers lost the basis of their power, which is organizational and defined in terms of the institutionalized leadership roles they pursued, their capacity to influence Portuguese politics subsequently was greatly impaired. This applies as much to Otelo Saraiva de Carvalho, once a popular leftwing officer, as it does to António Ramalho Eanes, the military president who more than any other single individual was responsible for the military's disengagement from political power. In both cases, once these men separated themselves from the military institution of which they had been an integral part and embarked on political careers of their own, their significance in the nation's political life rapidly declined.

In order to place Portuguese experience in this area in the wider comparative setting it so deserves, I would suggest using three variables. Combined, they offer an explanatory framework for the changing role of the military in Portuguese politics. First, there is the political choice factor—how military leaders have exercised their options at crucial junctures in the flow of national politics. Equally important is the development of political consciousness in the officer corps—an unequal process whereby a new sense of professional identity and commitment to social action reached some sectors before it did others. Lastly, but no less significantly, the institutionalization of competitive party politics stands out. Since the term "institutionalization" can be used in a variety of ways, it should be understood here that, applied to partisan politics, it refers to the process whereby the dominant political leadership tacitly agrees to abide by majority preferences expressed at the ballot box and by rules developed for channeling political conflict, regardless of political outcomes.

In the Portuguese context the formal statement of the agreement to establish a democratic regime is the Constitution of 1976. A "settlement" of sorts among the groups contending for power, it was intended from the beginning to be a transitional document within which concrete provision was made for reopening debate over the nature of the state and the arrangements by which it was to be governed in 1981.[1] This imperfect blending of principles derived from constitutional practice in Western democracies, notably France and the United Kingdom, with those of state socialism reflected the nature of the settlement reached in 1976. Only later (in 1989), once questions of military involvement in politics had been resolved and an accommodation between the right and the left worked out, was it possible to renegotiate the nationalizations made at the high point of the revolution and to remove the clauses in the Constitution committing the nation to a socialist ideal.

Nevertheless, the way in which this Constitution was written established a framework for channeling political controvery and made possible revisions in 1982 and 1989 that facilitated the institutionalization of a democratic regime through a prolonged series of partial settlements. In this context it is important to see the initial draft of the Constitution as a mechanism through which an accord was being reached that further attempts to promote the revolutionary transformation of Portuguese society would cease, as well as additional efforts to dismantle the market economy and the private sector. A crucial part of these developments was mutual awareness that neither the right nor the left had the capacity to impose its model for state and society without triggering violent reaction from the opposing side. These formal rules thus represent a negotiated agreement among the major political forces that Portugal would follow the democratic route in consolidating a new regime. They provided for a semi-presidential parliamentary system consisting of a president, national assembly (to whom the prime minister and cabinet were accountable), and a revolutionary council (through which the military institution was represented, until this body was abolished in the constitutional revisions of August 1982).

Much maligned in Portugal, this constitution in its original form reflected actual political practice and the nature of the debate over who should rule in the mid-1970s: the social democrats, the president and his supporters to the left, or a center-right coalition? The important point to be established here is that this document provided a formal statement of the rules of the game by which all the major power contenders would abide from 1976 onwards in their recourse to the ballot box. Each of these political alignments and their leaders—Mário Soares, António

Ramalho Eanes, and Francisco Sá Carneiro—found it impossible to rule Portugal alone. To survive, each had to work out an accommodation with those excluded from power as well as with those with whom they shared decision-making authority. To function, the system required a three-way understanding among prime minister, president, and revolutionary council. Simultaneously, to continue to exercise political influence, each had to find a way to maintain support from within his own mass constituency. In time as political passions lessened, it was possible to begin to adjust this "settlement," through removal of the revolutionary council and, as political consensus move to the center, through the neutralization of the socialist precepts written into the constitution.

As presently constituted, the Portuguese political system represents a hybrid mixture of presidentialist and parliamentary democratic practices. On the one hand, its institutions function according to its own particular version of the division of powers principle and the concept of checks and balances inherent in presidential regimes of the U.S. type. On the other, it gives full expression to European parliamentary practices, which if permitted to dominate political discourse would have made democracy unworkable, in a stalemated and fractured society. Its checks and balances can be observed easiest by watching the cycles through which presidential power waxes and wanes. But, it should always be emphasized, the individual components, the institutional actors, and the balance of power achieved differ as markedly from the U.S. case as it does from the French or British.

The Setting

Throughout recent decades, civil-military relations have been shaped by three very different regime contexts: authoritarian, revolutionary, and democratic. To capture this dynamic it becomes important to understand in summary fashion the sequence of events that took place, who the principal actors were in each phase, and the outcomes produced.

The conspiratorial nature of military politics in the early 1970s was directly linked to the character of the old regime. Dating back to the early 1930s, Salazar's New State (*Estado Novo*) constituted one of the longest instances of dictatorial rule in Western experience. So well entrenched was the state António Salazar created that, when he was incapacitated in 1968 and later died in 1969, it was possible to continue the institutions of governance he created without him. One of his closest associates, Marcello Caetano, assumed the premiership amid great hopes of renewal and reform—only to discover that he was locked into a system so dominated by the cumulative weight of institutions and choices made by his mentor over the previous 40 years that he soon became its captive rather than its leader.

While Salazar established his primacy early on in the creation of this authoritarian system, it should be remembered that the military was always a crucial component. The coup that overthrew the parliamentary First Republic was a military initiative and for the next seven years, 1926-1933, Portugal was governed by a military dictatorship. It was in that setting that Salazar first entered the government as Finance Minister and subsequently rose to power as Prime Minister. But, throughout the life of the New State, even though Salazar established effective control over the military institution, individual military officers remained actively involved in the regime's bureaucratic politics. His supporters in the military were guaranteed positions within the regime, beginning with the Presidency of the Republic, while his opponents conspired unsuccessfully to overthrow the regime.[2]

Salazar's ability to retain power and override repeated attempts to overthrow him calls attention to three critical differences in how he and his successor Caetano ruled. First, Caetano was never able to exercise the absolute power that Salazar did. His rule coincided with a degree of economic growth in mainland Portugal and Angola with which the statist structures of the New State could not cope. Predicated on no-growth assumptions and the defense of a traditional society in the modern world through a strategy of isolation, Caetano and his governments faced an impossible task. Without the political power held by his Spanish counterparts, there was no way he could reform the regime from within and lead the country along the road to controlled democracy. Second, in order to attract the international capital needed to sustain Portuguese colonialism and to stimulate new forms of corporate capitalism in Portugal necessitated dismantling many of the barriers erected by Salazar which isolated domestic life from external influences and change. To these two conditions must be added a third: increasing pressure to cut human and materiel costs in Portuguese Africa—through either preparing the way for peaceful independence of all Portugal's African territories or reducing the scope of Portuguese sovereignty in order to retain control of core population and production centers under some sort of new imperial relationship.

As we now know so well, Caetano and his governments became immobilized by the issues confronting the regime. No real change in any of the core policy areas, except for cosmetic alterations, meant that pressures would continue to build until an explosion occurred. Whether one examined the increasingly pan-European orientation of the economy in continental Portugal, control of the citizenry through censorship and police action, or the African question, the conclusions were the same: pressures for change from within, recognition of the need to act but inability to do so, and avoidance of pressures from without.

While the principle of civilian control of the military institution was well established by Salazar, one must never forget that throughout the life of the New State Salazar moved from squelching one potential conspiracy to another. There were several critical moments during his rule when the regime might have collapsed, but Salazar was always able to outmaneuver his opposition. Hence these various coups-in-the-making came to naught.[3]

At the same time, although this particular pattern of military intervention took on attributes peculiar to the New State era, it was part of an older and more general style of politics focused around individual personalities and the cliques they commanded. Pre-1974 Portugal, whether authoritarian, republican or constitutional monarchy, was essentially a society of limited participation. Whether one operated in a more open political setting (in the case of the First Republic) or a closed one (during the New State), there was neither great difference in class background for political elites nor in the way political factions organized their support on the basis of restricted and privileged clienteles.[4] Obviously there were great differences along ideological lines and in the definition of who could participate in the political life of the two regimes. The point, however, is that mass politics—the mobilization of urban and rural non-elites—did not occur in Portugal on a sustained basis until 1974.

Given the closed nature of the Salazar dictatorship and the extensive use of police power, opposition cliques and factions became very difficult to identify and to evaluate in terms of their membership and the extent of their support. To take two of the more visible examples, both Humberto Delgado (an activist military officer in open opposition to the Salazar regime) and Alvaro Cunhal (the secretary-general of the Portuguese Communist Party, PCP) served as important rallying points for protest movements. When mass demonstrations did take place in pre-1974 Portugal, as was the case in Delgado's 1958 campaign when Salazar temporarily relaxed controls, the response evoked and the techniques utilized were those of "populism." The focal point for these movements were the individual and his personal appeal to large numbers of people in urban areas, not the effectiveness of political organizations involving large groups. These patterns of politics emerged all the more clearly in 1974 and continued to appeal to major segments of the population, but quickly waned after 1976 as political parties provided a more effective organizational framework through which to mobilize large numbers of people.[5]

In this regard pre-1974 Portugal differed little from the forms of political mobilization found in other societies on the eve of mass politics. Between 1910 and 1974 instances of random mobilization followed the pattern of emotional appeals to an urban public in the major cities where large numbers could be brought together in public meetings. Throughout this era rural Portugal, where the majority of the population resided, remained outside formally constituted politics unless one was a local notable.

Under Caetano, as the New State declined in its ability to respond to the policy issues before it, two conspiratorial military movements got underway during the last half of 1972. These events followed two years of economic reform centered largely on the mainland during which the illusion of change was the greatest. On taking power as premier in 1971, Caetano recruited into his government a group of young technocrats (*homens novos*) with the hope that they would accomplish in Portugal what Franco's technocrats had accomplished a decade earlier. While these men did represent a new generation (a *camada nova*) and had the skills necessary to reform the economy, by the end of 1971 it was clear that their scope of action was extremely limited. Despite their advocacy of the view that Portugal's future lay in Europe, the older generation of military officers, civilian bureaucrats, and investors in Portuguese Africa used their power and prestige to ensure sustained commitment to the maintenance of a Portuguese presence in Africa and defense of the colonial status quo.

The old regime's uncompromising commitment to retaining sovereignty over all Portuguese territory in Africa saddled the military with an impossible task. They were obliged not only to maintain order and security throughout the whole of Angola, but also to defend the entire length of Mozambique's coast and its major communication links with inland Africa. To this was added the obligation of guaranteeing a Portuguese presence as well in the hinterland of Guinea-Bissau. In the decade following the outbreak of guerrilla activity in Angola in 1961 and the near collapse of Portuguese authority in the north, near the border with Zaire, the military had succeeded in stabilizing the Angolan situation. Despite continued guerrilla incursions along the northern frontier and throughout the less populated interior, core rural and urban areas were considered safe territories and the economy was booming. In Mozambique (east Africa), the task was more difficult and the response less effective. But, similar policies were in place by the early 1970s. Even there, irregardless of the logistical problems in protecting Portuguese enclaves in the north and in the center, especially the perimeter surrounding the Cabora Bassa dam project, military action was sufficient to protect productive urban and rural areas concentrated in the south and extending northward to the center of the colony. In contrast, Guinea-Bissau, thousands of miles to the north and west of these territories, presented no advantages whatsover. Attempts on the part of the military to convince civilian authorities to negotiate an exit there evoked instead the fear that a waning of Portuguese commitment anywhere would place the whole colonial project in jeopardy.

In hindsight, given the rigidities of regime policy toward Guinea-Bissau and awareness within the military institution of the futility of the effort as well as the costs in human lives, it is not all surprising that the origins of the discontent which produced the Movement of the 25th of April (the *Movimento 25 de Abril*) should lie in the shared experiences of the Guinea campaign. Since the commonality of these experiences are better known in discussions of the radicalization of the junior officers, what warrants emphasis here is that these perspectives belonged to older, senior officers as well and were linked to a second conspiratorial movement. General António Sebastião de Spínola was, after all, field commander in Guinea before he returned to Lisbon to head the

Portuguese General Staff (the Estado Maior Geral das Forças Armadas, EMGFA). Once back in Lisbon and in closer communication with other generals and senior officers, who had long supported the regime and shared in common African field experience (for example, Kaúlza de Arriaga and Jaime and Silvino Silvério Marques), Spínola and his allies moved closer and closer to the conclusion that the Caetano regime would have to be replaced by force before all was lost.

Two landmarks stand out in the evolution of conservative disaffection: the publication of Spínola's book (*Portugal e o Futuro*) and the ill-fated March 1974 right-wing military movement to replace Caetano. The former brought before the Portuguese public Spínola's scheme for the resolution of the African question, through negotiated political independence for the African territories, the creation of a commonwealth of Portuguese-speaking nations, and the retention for the present of Angola and Mozambique as integral parts of Portuguese territory. The latter (the failed March coup) closed off the possibility of a resolution of the crisis by intervention from the right and their removal of Caetano in order to bring about a negotiated solution to the African question.

From that point forward, the movement within the Armed Forces to oust Caetano shifted into the hands of junior officers. It was they who organized the coup that brought an end to Caetano and the New State on April 25, 1974. Originally called the Captains' Movement, its leaders soon adopted the name "The Armed Forces Movement" (the Movimento das Forças Armadas, MFA) to create the image of broad support throughout the military institution for their actions. This movement had two aspects: increasing recognition by its adherents that they were fighting wars which could not be won, and salary and rank grievances. Junior officers were the ones on whom the greatest pressures fell in fighting the guerrilla movements. Many were directly engaged in open combat; some flew planes of World War II vintage that were intended to support ground operations; others built and maintained forts in zones of intense guerrilla activity and moved the native population into fortified settlements. Whatever their particular tasks, all were subjected to and expected to use the propaganda identified with the regime's position (most notably the image of a multiracial society that separated Portuguese experience from that of other Europeans). Over time these field conditions coupled with rotation between Africa and the metropole produced a situation where more and more captains and majors became aware that their own individual discontentment was shared by a large number of military men.

If there was any ideology identified with the MFA, it was not specifically Marxist. Rather theirs was the language of protest which discovered in the popular literature of liberation identified with France's Algerian war and the guerrilla movements in Portuguese Africa themes they could relate to. Frequently termed "Marxist" by the popular press which zeroed in on Portugal after April 25, the MFA contained few adherents who really had read Marx and Lenin and almost no one who was well versed in left ideology in the sense that Portuguese Communist Party members were. Phrases, labels, terms were drawn from the civilian ideological left because they gave expression to sentiments these men felt. Yet most were "left" only in the sense that they opposed the regime: the social, economic, and political conditions of oppression that it had created at home and in Africa; its insensitivity to the pressures on and the needs of the military institution.

Professional grievances were just as important as those related to the wider political system. For years, discussion had taken place regarding the need to upgrade salaries paid to junior officers, but the Caetano government had remained adamant that it was unwilling to make across-the-board adjustments. The arguments presented were that the junior officers were badly underpaid in comparison to the salaries of the senior officers, not to mention the much higher wages paid to civilian professionals in general; also, that most of the responsibility for fighting in Africa rested on their shoulders. The cumulative effect of new employment opportunities for professionals in civilian jobs, low salaries for junior officers, and extended assignments in Africa in isolated places under hardship conditions produced a situation where by the early 1970s fewer and fewer men found military careers attractive.[6]

By 1972 the shortage of junior officers for assignments in Africa had become critical. Faced with this situation and aware that the draft was producing sufficient numbers of recruits to meet overall troop requirements, the Caetano government pressed to fill these vacancies by blanketing into the officer corps men from outside the career service. To some extent provisions already existed for giving recruits (milicianos) long-term career opportunities within a schema differentiating among *praças* (enlisted men), *sargentos*, and *oficiais*. Subject to proper training through the Military Academy and stints in field schools (*estágios nas Escolas Prácticas*), sargentos could be advanced to the career officer corps (the *quadro permanente de oficiais*). What military officers objected to was the lack of respect on the part of civilian policy makers for existing procedures, the number of *milicianos* whom it would blanket into the officer corps without sufficient preparatory training, and continuing insensitivity to the need for readjustments of pay scales and benefits for middle-range and lower-ranking officers. The attempt on the part of Caetano to resolve this situation by fiat through Decree No. 353/73 (July 1973) raised widescale objection from within the armed forces, so great that he was forced to rescind it with another decree in August, No. 409/73. By then Caetano's position was irretrievable.

Senior officers such as General Francisco Costa Gomes (whom Caetano named as Spínola's replacement as head of the EMGFA after his attempted coup) and General Spínola openly sided with the grievances of the captains and majors, protesting the Caetano government's actions and pressing for wage and benefit increases. Most of those affected by these actions reached the conclusion not only that a military victory in Africa was impossible but also that the incumbent regime was singularly insensitive to military needs and operations in defending the country's overseas interests. Thus, from late 1973 onward, it became increasingly a question not of whether there would be a coup but by whom and when. Even Caetano himself by early 1974 gave into a feeling of hopelessness in finding an exit from the immobilism gripping his government and sensed that military action was forthcoming.

MFA Dominance of the Revolution

Although Spínola served as symbolic head of the April 25 Movement and became the new President of the Republic, the junior officers in command were not the least moderate in their demands. Their goals were liquidation of empire, democratization of the entire nation (and that included the armed forces as well), dismantlement of the institutions of the old regime, and removal of its supporters from all positions of power, political as well as economic. In such a context neither Spínola nor anyone else espousing limited reform had a place. But theirs was a minority position within the military institution as well as in civil society. Hence, capturing control of the state apparatus and the major centers of economic power became an immediate priority. The spontaneity with which large numbers of people embraced the revolution obscured this fact, as did the rapid emergence of a new generation of political party leaders, without ties to the New State and with a strong commitment to the creation of a new society. Throughout the summer of 1974 it was not at all clear in which direction the revolution would move. The initial governments, in which power was shared between a military junta and a council of ministers, reflected this tentative mixture of moderates and radicals.[7]

Within the military institution the MFA confronted a situation where their movement remained an amorphous entity and where many if not most of the officers and enlisted men under their command were conservative rather than revolutionary in their political orientations. However, in the aftermath of the coup, few of these men wished to take strong stances. To protest against individual MFA actions made one vulnerable to accusations of fascism, the label attached to actions and structures of the old regime. Caught in the dilemma of sympathy with the original coup in its displacement of the Caetano government from power, yet uncomfortable with the increasingly radical rhetoric and actions of the younger officers, these men for the most part remained on the margins and attempted to the extent possible to go about their jobs as usual. With most of the senior military sidelined because of their identification with the old regime, a power vacuum emerged within the military institution which the MFA moved to fill.

During the summer following the coup, Spínola served as a real check on MFA aspirations—given his responsibility for serving as liaison between military and civilian authorities. As the MFA moved leftward, Spínola made it clear that he opposed their desire to liquidate Portugal's empire and that he had aligned himself with civilian forces opposed to further radicalization of the revolution. MFA officers, in turn, were able to isolate him by linking his name with the forces of reaction. However, before Spínola could be forced out, MFA officers recognized the need to give greater institutional form to their movement and to establish a way to ensure coordinated action. For this purpose they created two organs: a policy-making body called the Council of Twenty (*Conselho dos 20*) and a deliberative organ, the Council of 200 (*Conselho dos 200*). During these months a second policy-making body made its appearance: the Supreme Council of the MFA (the *Conselho Superior do MFA*). Sometimes it was synonymous with the Council of Twenty; more often it was not. Adding to further institutional confusion was the fact that not only did older state policy-making structures continue to operate (the Presidency of the Republic and the Council of Ministers), but there also were newer organs created to emphasize the coalition character of forces opposed to the New State and in favor of democratization, the Junta of National Salvation and the Council of State.

Mobilization of civilian groups on the center and the right for the purpose of holding a large public meeting in Lisbon on September 28 (to demonstrate their support for Spínola) degenerated into rumors that a countercoup was in preparation. To squelch that possibility the MFA leadership moved quickly to contain that demonstration, to block access to Lisbon from outside, and to force Spínola and the remaining conservative officers out of power. In the meantime, MFA control of crucial government positions had already increased. On the Junta of National Salvation they had two representatives, Vice Admirals José Batista Pinheiro de Azevedo and António Alva Rosa Coutinho. In the Second Provisional Government, that is the second cabinet of ministers appointed on July 7, military representation had been increased to seven and a MFA officer, António Vasco dos Santos Gonçalves, named as prime minister.

Taking advantage of this situation, another MFA officer, Otelo Saraiva de Carvalho, moved into a position of great power and considerable public visibility. As head of the Lisbon military region (the *Governo Militar de Lisboa*) and commander of Continental Operations (*Comando Continental, COPCON*), Otelo had control of troops in the nation's capital.[8] Faced with his opposition, conservatives and moderates had to resign: General Spínola as president; Generals Carlos Galvão de Melo, Manuel Diogo Neto, and Jaime Silvério Marques as junta members; and Colonel Mário Firmino Miguel and Major Sanches Osório as cabinet ministers. With their exit went the last of the senior officials who had survived the coup as creditable public figures.

The MFA was now in full command of the military institution and was at the front of the revolutionary government. Joining Vasco Gonçalves and Otelo, and as replacements for those ousted, were Brigadier General Carlos Fabião and Lieutenant Colonel Lopes Pires in the Army; Colonel Pinho Freire and Lieutenant Colonel Mendes Dias in the Air Force. The sole senior officer to survive was Costa Gomes and, given his compliancy with MFA leadership, he became an ideal replacement for Spínola as president.

From their position of dominance of the military institution, the MFA leadership moved to restructure authority relations from within. By late fall the Coordinating Commission of the MFA with its 25 members had become the effective policy-making body and the Council of Twenty, less important. Complementing this change was the move to open up representation with the Council of 200 by removing the requirement of participation in the April movement and permitting the election of any officer on the basis of a majority within his respective branch of the armed forces. Yet none of this followed clear-cut lines and considerable debate within and without the military institution continued, in the same way that open competition for power and position was occurring within the civilian arena among the newly formed parties and their leaders.

The second attempt to end MFA leadership of the revolution on March 11, 1975, centered around military rather than civilian action. It was even more of a failure than the attempt to mobilize civilians in public protest the previous September. Thoroughly discredited by his agreement to serve as new head of government should the coup succeed, Spínola had no choice but to flee the country. In the aftermath, radical officers moved quickly to consolidate their position. They replaced the previous plurality of decision-making organs with a single supreme executive authority, the Council of the Revolution. Incorporated into the Council were the Junta of National Salvation, the Coordinating Commission of the MFA, and the Council of Twenty. In addition, responsibility for determining military policy was shifted from the EMGFA to the Council. Under these arrangement there was to be no question that the Council of Ministers, now in the form of the Fourth Provisional Government, was a subordinate body, charged with the execution of day-to-day governmental affairs. Within the military institution further impetus was given to isolation of officers not openly sympathetic with the Armed Forces Movement. To ensure MFA control and identification of the MFA with the armed forces as a whole, the MFA leadership gave the Council of 200 the name of Armed Forces Assembly and expanded its representation to 240. Under the new arrangements one no longer had to be a commissioned officer to serve as delegate;

sergeants and enlisted men also could be elected. The army was assigned 120 representatives (with 60 places allotted to commissioned officers, 30 to noncommissioned officers, and 20 to enlisted men,) while the navy and the air force received 60 each (with a similar internal ratio within their ranks).

In cooperation with the left political parties, the MFA moved to guarantee the revolutionary transformation of Portugal. This was the most radical phase of the revolution and it was to extend from March through the end of August 1975. Nationalization of banks, insurance companies, and major firms owned by Portuguese interests occurred. Complementing this were spontaneous popular movements whereby workers seized control of firms, as their owners fled the country or declared bankruptcy, and residents of poor neighborhoods organized housing commissions to occupy any vacant housing they could identify. In the countryside the MFA sought to give further impetus to the occupation of the land and the formation of agricultural cooperatives that already had occurred in the Alentejo by organizing revolutionary units under military auspices, the *Comissões Dinamizadoras*. Their rhetoric led them to believe that once the peasantry throughout Portugal received the message of revolution with its emphasis on liberation and people's organizations, they would rise up and join the armed forces in their struggle to achieve revolutionary transformations. As is now well known, that illusion provoked a tremendous reaction throughout the small-landowning peasantry north of the Tagus. Rather than acceptance, these teams of militants encountered determined resistance throughout the north, where as mass mobilization took place people identified themselves with organizations opposed to the revolution.

The Emergence of Military Factions

With conservatives and moderates in the military and civil society isolated, if not ousted from positions of import, the MFA embarked on a policy of moving the country toward state socialism. That goal, however, engendered tremendous debate within the MFA just as it did in the larger society. At that point civil-military alliances became an important ingredient of the revolution and the armed forces ceased to operate as a cohesive entity. During what came to be known as the "hot summer" (*verão quente*) of 1975, one could identify four distinct left alignments within the military and the beginnings of what was then a still ill-defined but increasingly important regrouping of moderates.

The major faction centered around Vasco Gonçalves, premier since the previous summer; hence, their designation as *gonçalvistas*. Included in this faction were Captain Ferreira de Macedo, Lieutenant Captain Carlos Contreiras, Captain Martins Guerrero, First Lieutenant Miguel Judas, Colonel João Varela Gomes, Colonel Ramiro Correia, and Vice-Admiral Rosa Coutinho. These men favored formation of a left alliance with the Portuguese Communist Party (PCP) and the pro-Communist MDP/CDE.[9]

Vasco Gonçalves' own particular political style was filled with populist rhetoric and his program for building socialism within Portugal lacked coherence, but this was not necessarily the case with the other officers. Judas, Varela Gomes, and Rosa Coutinho were much more sophisticated ideologically. Thus, while many of the MFA officers had a poor understanding of Marx and Lenin and what building socialism really meant, these men recognized the need for developing a more disciplined mass movement and were ready to work with the PCP-MDP/CDE alliance.

As the MFA's representative in Angola, Rosa Coutinho played a crucial role in turning over power to Agostinho Neto and his Marxist MPLA (the Movimento Popular para a Libertação de Angola). Working together they isolated the other liberation movements which were much less amenable to their concept of a socialist Angola. The argument was that the MPLA alone was equipped with the organization and the men to staff an independent government, but one cannot neglect the ideological predisposition Rosa Coutinho and the MFA officers supporting his course of action had for the MPLA's program and its vision for the liberation of the country. So close was Rosa Coutinho's association with the MPLA during the transition and so visible was his action that he in particular became the *bete noir* of the Portuguese right, especially those who had returned from Africa (the *retornados*). This is the origin of the epithet attached to his name, the "Red Admiral."

Counterbalancing Vasco Gonçalves and those officers favoring the construction of a popularly-based left alliance were Otelo and another group of MFA officers: Commander Jorge Correia Jesuíno, Major

Aventino Teixeira, Captain Duarte Into Soares, General Morais da Silva, and Admiral Pinheiro de Azevedo. While they too favored forming a broadly based military-civilian alliance, they differed from the previous group in their determination to have the military retain an upper hand. If Cuba could be said to be the more appropriate model for Vasco Gonçalves, Judas, Varela Gomes, and Rosa Coutinho—during late spring and early summer 1975, the Lisbon press identified such men as Otelo, Jesuíno, and Pinheiro de Azevedo with what was called the Peruvian option: the concept of a left-oriented military movement which would lead and direct the revolution.

While Vasco Gonçalves pursued political action and civilian mobilization, Otelo made use of the troops and the military organization at his disposal. COPCON became the sponsor for the Comissões Dinamizadoras. The Fifth Division assumed responsibility for coordinating and developing the MFA's program through an organ called the Comissão Coordinadora do Programa do MFA. That office published the MFA's bimonthly newspaper, *Movimento 25 de Abril: Boletim Informativo das Forças Armadas*. Complementing these activities was the use of radio, television, and press releases favorable to the MFA. Through his position as minister and head of the newly formed Ministério da Comunicação Social, Jesuíno provided an important support for the MFA cause. This particular ministry was a spin-off from the old regime's information and press services in the prime minister's own ministry, the Presidência do Conselho, and continued the previous government's practice whereby the state dominated and directly controlled much of the Portuguese media. Insofar as the newly formed political parties were concerned, Otelo and his group had their closest ties with the Maoist MRPP (Movimento Revolucionário Popular Português) and the PRP-BR (Partido Revolucionário do Proletariado-Brigadas Revolucionárias), a Marxist organization committed to the use of violence to achieve its goals.

It is important to emphasize here the difference between these two alignments on the left. While the former involved an effort to build a revolutionary civil-military coalition, the latter was centered in the military and maintained autonomy from the civilian groups with which it was in contact. Insofar as the informed public in Portugal is concerned, however, this relationship was not clarified until considerably later, in the controversy which emerged in late 1980 over the legal testimony (*depoimento*) given by a former PRP militant and brigade member, seized after one of the bank assaults. Aware of the anarchic nature of these movements and their proclivity for violence, Otelo attempted to disassociate himself from them.[10] But to his detriment, he did not finally break with them until fall 1975. By then it was too late: The revolutionary brigades had already received arms through COPCON and there was no way he could convince military moderates that he was not actively engaged in fomenting revolution.

The third group of military officers consisted of those who were diametrically opposed to the previous two groups, especially in their recourse to demonstrations and violence if necessary to achieve their goals. Its major proponents, Major Ernesto de Melo Antunes and Brigadier General Vasco Lourenço, argued that the original intent of the April 25 Movement was to establish social democracy in Portugal. In their eyes such actions precluded what was indispensable to the consolidation of socialism in Portugal, victory at the ballot box and the creation of a democratic majority. Their ties were closest with the newly formed Portuguese Socialist Party (PS). Before the events of March 11, this alignment probably reflected the majority sentiment of those identified with the MFA, but as political divisions became more rigid, their position became less and less tenable. As the far-left press and militants increased their attacks on the social democrats for being counterrevolutionary in character, these officers sought to carve out a more distinct position. They insisted that the proper course for the revolution to follow would be to identify Portugal less with the ideological controversies characteristic of the European left and much more closely with the developing world outside Europe. The label the press used to identify them accordingly was *terceiro-mundistas*—pro-Third-Worlders—because of their sympathies with the Non-Aligned Movement.

The last MFA group was in reality a residual category; it involved men not comfortable with any of the above positions, but equally left in their orientation. Exemplifying this stance were Lieutenant Colonel Manuel Franco Charais and General Carlos Fabião. However, as political forces polarized in September 1975, they lined up with Otelo's position (this was Fabião's case) or that of Melo Antunes (as occurred with Charais).

The rapid movement of events during summer 1975, the plurality of civilian and military actors vying for leadership positions, and the way in which the international mass media zeroed in on Portugal as a social revolution in the making served to obscure a very important fact. The MFA did not represent majority sentiment within the military institution, despite the image it sought to build. To conduct the purges necessary to turn the armed forces into a solid support for building the kind of socialist republic they desired required both control and discipline which the MFA officers by the very nature of their own movement were incapable of providing. The only disciplined left organization in the country was that headed by Alvaro Cunhal, the PCP. Its ties with the MFA were neither close enough nor strong enough to penetrate the military institution to the degree required to bring about such a transformation.

As was the case with civil society, it took much longer for the more conservative majority of officers and enlisted men to organize themselves. There were several reasons why. Most of them agreed with the original MFA program and had supported the coup. Those openly identified with the old regime had already lost credit and had been forceably retired; besides, they were a minority. Second, these men considered themselves to be professionals and as such respect for the existing hierarchy of authority was well ingrained in them. While they did not necessarily agree with the policies of the military institution's new commanders, they continued to follow orders. As long as social-democratic perspectives dominated, they felt their positions would be respected and they honestly believed that the MFA's commitment to democracy was sincere. As the revolution moved leftward, extremists took command, and the threat of left authoritarianism became a distinct possibility, disaffection grew. More importantly, with the radicalization of the revolution, it became more and more clear that internal order and hierarchy within the armed forces was disintegrating. The idea of democratic representation within the military institution was producing a situation in which as enlisted men and non-commissioned officers were coming to determine the proper course of action, commissioned officers found themselves more and more on the sidelines. Finally, these men were a great deal like their civilian counterparts in that these people were the least likely to join in concerted action. Intense individualism and hostility toward partisan politics combined to delay the formation of group consciousness. But under the pressure of events and with the realization that individual survival required collective action, they organized themselves in the same way a new civilian center and right with a mass base began to emerge in that same period.

Like the MFA radicals who attempted to consolidate their control over the military institution and the government after March 11, the military moderates were a small group of officers. Beginning as an informal group in September and October, they soon organized the movement that took the form of the November 25 coup that displaced the MFA from power. In this respect they were not a great deal different from previous military history with its legacy of conspiratorial movements, some successful, most failures. They differed from their immediate predecessors, however, in that their protest and action quickly rallied majority sentiment behind them and the officer corps for the most part willingly complied with their new orders. So rapid was this reversal in collective sentiment within the armed forces that MFA adherents suddenly found themselves isolated, for few were the cases where enlisted men were willing to stand behind them. While Melo Antunes, a leading representative of the social-democratic faction, played a crucial role in protesting revolutionary excesses, he no less than others in the MFA found himself in a minority and without effective power after November 25, 1975. Articulating the demand that the MFA leadership return to the original April 25 program, he circulated a document within the Council of the Revolution calling for a recommitment to democracy. Important at the time, it was quickly superseded by the events which followed.

The Portuguese left, civilian as well as military, had become victims of their own rhetoric. Many honestly believed, as did not a few foreign observers, that in an appeal to the barracks in a moment of crisis troops would rise up in defense of the revolution. November 25 was that crisis. Frantic appeals were made. Militants outside the military invoked the slogan "Soldados Unidos Vencerão" (Soldiers United Will Conquer). Yet when the chaos subsided, it was not the MFA officers who were in command, but military moderates.[11]

Reign of the Moderates

From 1976 until the end of the 1980s, when public remembrances of the revolutionary era largely ceased, ceremonies held each November 25 became nearly as important as those on April 25. For military moderates and conservatives the November date symbolized the containment of the radicals, especially those identified with the alliance between left officers and the PCP, and recommitment to the April 25 Movement's original promise of democracy and civilian rule. It was also a time when the military leadership made frequent reference to the military's role as guarantor of Portugal's new democracy and its subordination to civil authority.

If military radicalism is to be identified with Vasco Gonçalves and left-wing populism with Otelo, then it is António Ramalho Eanes who symbolizes the more moderate stances taken by the military since 1975, its support for a democratic regime and subordination to civil authority, and its withdrawal from politics. First elected president in June 1976 and reelected in December 1980, when he turned power over to Mário Soares after a decade in office, he left behind a vastly different military institution. Standing between the left and the right, he and his supporters depoliticized the military institution, first converting it into a moderating force in Portuguese society and then leading it out a politics through marginalizing the Council of the Revolution and finally cooperating in its abolition in 1982. As president of the republic and commanding officer of the EMGFA, he used his dual authority to reinforce the use of the ballot box and elections as the appropriate mechanisms through which political controversy should be channeled. In this capacity he sought to make certain that all major interests would be adequately represented (and this included that part of the left to whom the right would deny legitimacy as participants) while he oversaw the reorganization of the armed forces into a small peacetime organization more thoroughly integrated into the North Atlantic Treaty Organization.

During his first term of office, Eanes was an active participant in the three-way sharing of executive power that symbolized the political settlement reached among the major contestants for power. As president, he emphasized and reinforced his role as the representative of the entire electorate. This he contrasted with the more partisan role played by prime ministers and cabinets, accountable to the Assembly of the Republic and reflective of continually shifting party alignments and supports, and the role of the Council of the Revolution, as the institutionalization of the April 25 Movement and its military constituency.   .

Still, one should not minimize the give and take that developed in Portuguese politics during these years and the attempts that Eanes made to assert presidential power. Each side pushed the new system to its limits and in turn had to recognize that survival of the new regime was contingent on the acceptance of its opposition. This was the pattern throughout Eanes' first five-year term of office. Initially Mário Soares, under the First and the Second Constitutional Governments, attempted to assert leadership through the Socialist Party only to discover that by working alone or in coalition he could not amass sufficient support to create a coherent program and sustain a government. With the collapse of the second Soares government in June 1978, a period ensued in which the President attempted to gain the upper hand by appointing a series of technocratic cabinets only to find that he could not effectively govern without majority support in the Assembly of the Republic and working with the political parties. New elections in October 1979 produced yet another alternative, a center-right Democratic Alliance led by Francisco Sá Carneiro. Reconfirmed in October 1980 parliamentary elections, Sá Carneiro led the attack to see if the center-right could produce a working majority by electing its candidate General António Soares Carneiro president in December. Sá Carneiro's death just before this second round of elections coupled with Eanes re-election served to send the same message: the center-right, just as was the case with the center-left and with advocates of a strong presidentialism, could not act alone.

At this point, with each of the major four parties—the PCP, the PS, the PSD, and the CDS—representing self-contained constituencies and a second presidential term ahead of him, Eanes put his efforts behind building the Portuguese presidency as an institution representing the nation as a whole, above and beyond existing party alignments. Seeing in his reelection a popular mandate, Eanes moved to disassociate his office from its ties with the military institution after 1980 and to reinforce his own identification with civilian rule. Stepping down as head of the Portuguese General Staff (EMGFA), he appointed a full-time military officer, General Melo Egídio, to that post. Backing up this appointment was establishment of the practice of naming civilians to the position of Defense Minister. First initiated when Sá Carneiro selected CDS vice-president Adelino Amaro da Costa, from this point forth the president and whoever filled the role of prime minister had a tacit understanding that the appointment would be a civilian. In order to achieve more effective implementation of this separation of civil and military authority, Eanes also reorganized his own office staff—located in administrative units known as his military and civilian households (the Casas Militar e Civil)—and appointed a trio of supporters to head the Army: Generals Amadeu Garcia dos Santos (former head of his military household), Lopes Alves (former Comandante Geral of the Policia de Segurança Pública, the PSP) and José Aparício (former PSP commander of the Lisbon district) as Chefe do CME (the Comando Maior do Exército), Vice-Chefe do CME, and adjutant to the Chefe, respectively.

A second priority was downgrading the Council of the Revolution and ultimately its abolition, in cooperation with civilian leaders when the constitution was amended in 1982. This was simply a continuation and acceleration of actions taken during his first presidency. For example, early on in November 1976, he imposed the requirement that one could not be both a member (*conselheiro*) of the Council and a military commander. The purpose in doing so was to remove what military moderates considered to be one of the causes of military intervention in politics during the 1974-1976 period: the appointment of regional commanders (those generals, five in number, with troops directly at their disposal) to political positions. In the interim, while the Council continued to function as a viable entity and as a source of power, Eanes made a point of the fact that he presided over the Council exclusively in his capacity as President of the Republic, reduced the role of the elected members of the Council, and worked primarily with the heads of the three branches of the armed forces, positions filled by men identified with him.

At this point there is no reason to review further specific actions taken and appointments made during Eanes' second term to separate military and civilian affairs and to remove the military from politics. The legacy of this work is represented in the status of civil-military relations today, under the presidency of Mario Soares. By the time the transfer of power took place in 1986, from Eanes as a former military officer to Soares as the first civilian president since the collapse of the First

Republic in 1926, depoliticization of the military and subordination of the military institution to civil authority had been fixed. In light of the crisis era, 1974-1976, what is remarkable about this sequence of events is the extent to which Eanes and his supporters succeeding in changing the course of military action decisively, first neutralizing the revolutionary left and then making certain that, whatever their political orientation might be, Portuguese officers would no longer play a role in politics without retiring from active military service and separating themselves from the men under their command.

Conclusion

The fact that Eanes' policies were not easily implemented and that a relatively short period of time has passed since the military was so actively engaged in Portuguese politics should not lead to skepticism about the extent of the changes achieved. What occurred in military affairs matches the transformation of civilian affairs. To have moved so quickly from right authoritarianism to the brink of revolutionary upheaval to pluralist democracy is indeed an accomplishment in the contemporary world that few nations can lay claim to. Consolidation of these new institutions, military and civilian, and the viability of Portugal's new democracy do remain vulnerable to external conditions. But this is mitigated by three factors: the commitment of the present generation of civilian and military elites to the consolidation of Portuguese democracy, be they right, center, or left in political orientation; the marginalization of the authoritarian right and left, and the integration of Portugal into Europe through the economic and political ties promoted by its entry into the European Economic Community. How this transformation was attained is the concern of the next chapter.

Notes

1. The term "settlement is adapated from the work of John Higley in which he develops the concept of "elite settlement" as an essential element in regime consolidation. See: Michael G. Burton and John Higley, "Elite Settlements," in *Texas Papers on Latin America*, No. 87-01

(Austin: Institute of Latin American Studies, University of Texas at Austin, 1987).

2. The primary sources regarding military participation in politics during the authoritarian era are: Douglas Wheeler, *A Ditadura Militar Portuguesa, 1926-1933* (Mém Martins: Publicações Europa-América, 1986) and his chapter "The Military and the Portuguese Dictatorship, 1926-1974: 'The Honor of the Army,'" in Lawrence S. Graham and Harry M. Makler (eds.), *Contemporary Portugal: The Revolution and Its Antecedents* (Austin: University of Texas Press, 1979).

3. For an excellent overview of this situation and an analysis of the various military coups attempted, some with success, most without, from the First Republic through the end of Salazar's rule, see the chapter by Douglas Wheeler in Graham and Makler.

4. Data confirming continuity in class background are provided by Philippe Schmitter in his chapter, "The 'Regime d'Exception' That Became the Rule: Forty-Eight Years of Authoritarian Domination in Portugal," in Graham and Makler.

5. An especially good discussion of this aspect of Portuguese politics is to be found in David L. Raby, "Populism and the Portuguese Left: From Delgado to Otelo," in Lawrence S. Graham and Douglas L. Wheeler (eds.), *In Search of Modern Portugal: The Revolution and its Consequences* (Madison: The University of Wisconsin Press, 1983).

6. For supporting data on enrollments and graduates consult my chapter on the military, "The Military in Politics: The Politicization of the Portuguese Armed Forces," in Graham and Makler, pp. 228-29.

7. Consistently after April 25 and until the formation of Sá Carneiro's Sixth Constitutional Government in 1979, the position of Defense Minister was reserved for a military officer who was given the responsibility of serving as liaison between military and civilian authorities. From this point forward, "government" (lower case) will be used to refer to any particular regime in power, while the term "Government" (upper case) will be used to refer to a particular governing team, consisting of a prime minister named by the president and the cabinet selected by that prime minister.

8. It was Saraiva de Carvalho's first name, Otelo, that the media used. From this point forward, rather than his family name, I will use "Otelo." This is the name by which he continues to be known in politics.

9. This party, the Movimento Democrático Português/Comissão Democrática Eleitoral, was an electoral alliance formed during the later years of the Salazar dictatorship. While it was in a position to occupy many of the local government posts vacated by the fall of the Caetano government, it was unable to develop a mass constituency of its own after 1974.

10. For a detailed account of this particular episode see the extended article published in the magazine section of *Expresso*, "Assaltantes de bancos eram do PRP e armados pelo COPCON," December 20, 1980, p. 2-R ff, and Isabel do Carmo's reply, "Isabel do Carmo explica-se ao Expresso," *Expresso*, January 24, 1981, pp. 11-12.

11. Those interested in a more detailed analysis of the revolution between 1974 and 1976, periodization of its major phases, and patterns of civil-military interaction during them might wish to consult my chapter on the military in, "The Military in Politics: The Politicization of the Portuguese Armed Forces," Graham and Makler.

3

Redefining the Role of the Military in a Democratic Portugal

The transformation of the military institution, from within, during the decade extending from 1976 to 1986 is one of the most important components of the Portuguese transition. Yet, it is probably the least well understood aspect of how Portugal has moved into the ranks of consolidated democratic regimes during the 1990s. Much better known and more widely understood, in comparative perspective, is the Spanish transition in which subordination of the military to civilian authority was accomplished quickly, dramatically, and overtly. Furthermore, in the creation and development of a civilian-dominated Defense Ministry Spain has come to match much more closely European patterns in the establishment of civilian oversight authority. Compared also to the relative ease of the Central European transitions, in which transferral of civilian oversight authority from Communist party officials to the new democratic leadership in Poland, the Czech and Slovak Republics, and Hungary took place without conflict, the Portuguese case stands apart and really has not been a part of the discourse over democratic transitions and consolidations.[1]

Had not certain military figures used their authority to reshape the military institution from within while new civil-military relations were being developed from without, the Portuguese transition to democracy would have been a much more tentative affair. This point is crucial in contrasting Portuguese experience with that of Brazil. While the Brazilian transition was made possible by the organization of a grassroots, civilian-based opposition movement and the military ultimately decided it was in its best interest institutionally to disengage from power, at no point has it forsaken any of its institutional prerogatives. At the moment there is no doubt about the support of the military leadership in Brazil for civilian-based democratic rule, despite all the problems with presidential leadership since the transition. But, in no way has the military placed itself under civilian control.[2] Even more dramatic is the case of the Angolan military and opposition paramilitary forces. While Angola remains a long way away from initiating its democratic transition, what is instructive once again is how little attention was given to internal military affairs in negotiating the peace accords. After the fact, now that there are serious difficulties on both sides in negotiating how a coalition government is to work in which the MPLA will have majority representation, there is general recognition that much more attention should have been given to effective demobilization of the MPLA military and UNITA paramilitary units, during the sixteen months elapsing from the signing of the peace accords to the holding of elections.

In accounting for how the role of the Portuguese military was redefined during the 1980s, the framework utilized in this chapter emphasizes the importance of distinguising between two decisive phases in the evolution of the military institution during these years. The first is movement away from the historic pattern of a politicized military, characterized by periodic subordination to "subjective" civilian controls and alternating cycles of incursion into politics, preceding and following the establishment of civilian regimes—both authoritarian and democratic. The second is consolidation of a new set of institutional arrangements designed to establish continuity in the disengagement of the military from political life, in which "objective" civilian controls have been established for the first time.[3] These two periods coincide with the first and the second terms of office of President António Ramalho Eanes, June 1976-December 1980 and January 1981-April 1986. By the time Mário Soares assumed the presidency in 1986 as Eanes' successor, the circle had been closed in the restructuring of civil-military relations.

While these patterns can be identified more easily in hindsight, they were not at all apparent as these adjustments were underway and accommodations were being made by each of the major actors. This is because they coincided with tremendous changes in all of Portuguese society in a relatively compressed period of time. Seen from this perspective, the decade 1976-1986 marks an era during which civil-military relations underwent decisive reformulation, and not without considerable trauma, as older institutional patterns were dismantled and new ones constituted.

The End of the Era of Subjective Military Controls

When António Ramalho Eanes first took office as president, following his election by a clear majority in June 1976, he did so as the military leader of a coup the previous November that had displaced military and civilian radicals from power and as Commander-in-Chief of the Portuguese Armed Forces. At that point in time, when one examined the military institution, what stood out was the extent to which it mirrored state and society. In 1976 Portugal was a country traumatized by revolution, characterized by considerable institutional disarray, and occupied by a people who in the majority now desired social peace and civil accord. The military institution in turn reflected these circumstances and attitudes.

The rapidity and the profundity of the changes with which the Portuguese were confronted in the decade 1966-1976 have since receded into the background, but they warrant remembering here in order to comprehend the desire that had emerged to resolve differences at the ballot box rather than through armed conflict. Just ten years earlier (1966) the state and the military had been so thoroughly imbued with the authoritarian values and the conservative patterns of social and political behavior dominant in Salazar's Portugal that any other projection beyond continuation of the prevailing power structure seemed idle speculation. Just five years earlier (1971) with Salazar dead and his heir apparent Caetano ensconced in power, it had not seemed inconceivable that the authoritarian regime known as the New State (Estado Novo) would continue intact for the foreseeable future. At that point, economic modernization was underway on the mainland in isolated pockets along the coast and containment of guerrilla insurgency seemed likely in Angola and no longer impossible in Mozambique. By 1976 only two years had lapsed since the April 25th coup led by junior officers that had opened up the country to revolutionary changes and brought independence to Portugal's overseas territories.

During that decade (1966-1976) three markedly different patterns of power and civil-military relations had predominated. But all shared in common the assumption that the military was a major stakeholder and participant in key decisions. The first consisted of conservative authoritarian rule in which a hierarchical, pre-World-War-II military establishment had used mass conscription and surplus World-War II

materiel to fight its African wars. The second entailed removal by force
of civilian and military leaders identified with the old order and their
replacement by civilian and military radicals caught up in the
revolutionary rhetoric of the April 25th Armed Forces Movement
(Movimento das Forças Armadas, MFA). Whereas the values identified
with the former stressed order, hierarchy, and an ethic of service and
compliance with directives, the latter stressed spontaneous commitment
to revolutionary ideals, decision making by representative assemblies of
workers and enlisted men, and freedom to experiment with the new
social relationships and communal associations that had emerged
overnight.

Those identified with the November 25, 1975, coup that displaced the
radicals from power had yet another set of values and a very different
concept of the place of the military within state and society. In the
absence of a more appropriate term, "moderates" will be used here to
refer to these men.[4] Caught between two eras, they belonged for the
most part to a largely silent generation, restricted in number, betwixt two
more vocal, more ideological, more militant generations. Comfortable
neither with the "ultras" of the Salazar years nor the "gonçalvistas" of
1974 and 1975, this generation of military officers favored a democratic
Portugal, freed from the burden of overseas colonies and committed to
modernization via entry into the European Community. If Admiral
Américo Tomás (president 1958-1974) epitomized the older generation of
military officers displaced by the 1974 coup, Otelo Saraiva de
Carvalho—the major charged with responsibility for taking control of the
military institution in the original plot to overthrow the Caetano
government—gave expression to the passion and rhetoric identified with
the Revolution of Flowers (the popular name given to the April 25th
movement and symbolizing its use of carnations in rifles, as images for
the new society to be built). In turn, it is General António Ramalho
Eanes who best represents the military generation that came to the fore
at the end of 1975 and played such an important role in the changes
undertaken over the next decade (1976-1986).[5]

The situation Eanes encountered in 1976 required decisive action.
The two preceding years of turmoil had so politicized the military
institution that it had lost most of its coherency as an organization
capable of protecting national security interests, be they external or
internal. Independence of the overseas territories had removed the need

for mass conscription and for a military institution capable of sustaining warfare under primitive conditions. The changes incorporated during the reign of the radicals had dismantled the old military hierarchy to such an extent that, despite the swing to the right in late 1975, there was no possibility of a counterrevolution, in the sense of returning the old guard to power. Yet those advocating reinvolvement of the military in politics were as numerous as ever, albeit now in the defense of political democracy and private property. Political alignments on the left, the right, and the center all represented different constellations of civilian and military leaders. Seen in organizational terms, by this point the military as an identifiable institution distinct from civilian society had largely ceased to exist. The prerevolutionary divisions between the services and within them between officers and enlisted men had disintegrated further into warring factions at odds with each other because of fundamental political and ideological differences.

Given this situation, Eanes and his supporters in the military agreed on one basic principle: If a democratic regime was to be built and admission to the European Community (EC) attained, the armed forces would have to disengage from direct involvement in politics, adhere to new professional norms, and reestablish their organizational integrity. The latter objective emphasized that, despite individual differences, the loyalty of the officer corps must be first and foremost to the military institution. The new national reality confronting them was the possibility of a single geopolitical focus for the first time in centuries—the Continental Portugal, Azores, Madeira triangle. Such a focus would require active participation in the North Atlantic Treaty Organization (NATO), enhancement of the navy and the air force, and reduction of the influence traditionally enjoyed by the army, followed by the latter's reorganization into a much smaller fighting force oriented to the defense of Portugal's Atlantic perimeter. To accomplish this, the armed forces as a whole would have to be modernized in accord with standards set for other NATO members. But, the institutional disarray with which they were confronted and the intense emotions surrounding the personalities and symbols identified with the revolution made this an extraordinarily difficult task. How such policy objectives could be implemented were as delicate a matter in internal military affairs as any of the major domestic issues facing civilian politicians committed to constituting a democratic system that would endure and a market economy that would work.

The first step involved dismantling structures identified with the MFA and reestablishing the supremacy of the General Staff of the Armed Forces (the Estado Maior Geral das Forças Armadas, EMGFA). From the time of his election as president the end of June 1976 up until the initiation of his second term of office in 1981, Eanes played a dual role: commander-in-chief of the armed forces as president of the republic—a role he conceptualized in civilian terms—and head of the military institution in his capacity as "chefe" of the General Staff of the Armed Forces (CEMGFA).

In this setting, as pointed out earlier, the Constitution of 1976 functioned more as a political settlement among the major contenders for power under a newly constituted democratic regime, rather than as a basic charter intended to establish a constitutional framework for future democratic governance. Again, people as much in Portugal as outside—in their constant reference to the Constitution's hybrid character and the need for its amendment or replacement—have forgotten this quality. This was a constitution ratified not by popular mandate but by parties elected by popular vote to the Constituent Assembly. In the final vote, the nature of this settlement was reflected in the vote in favor of the document by all the parties in attendance, except for 16 deputies identified with the new right in Portuguese politics, the CDS. Likewise, the tripartite division of authority among the Presidency of the Republic, the Council of the Revolution (in which leading military officers identified with the revolution were represented), and the Assembly of the Republic (with its prime minister and council of ministers) reflected the nature of the settlement reached. Leaders in the activities of each of these organizations had different concepts of how executive and legislative relations should function. Thus, it was only in the course of time—after each contingent had come to grips with the fact that it alone could not rule successfully—that these new relationships were to be worked out in the give and take of a bargaining and competitive style of politics.

Considerable conflict and uncertainty followed as a consequence of this particular division of authority. Each of those commanding leading positions in the Office of the President, the Assembly of the Republic, and the Council of the Revolution had a major stake in determining the course of action to be pursued by the state. By definition, this produced a fluid situation, with some advocating presidentialism; others, parliamentarianism, and still others, lasting military influence. Eanes, as much as any of the other principal figures, became actively involved in the attempt to influence the content of these new structures for governance. He, no less than his competitors, did not consider this initial tripartite separation of powers to be permanent, in the course of building a new democracy.

In the context of a divided military and numerous civilian-military alignments, command over the armed forces, assertion of civilian authority, and disengagement of the military from politics were not matters that could be decided simply by fiat. Each major action taken required negotiation, considerable jockeying back and forth, and adjustment to countervailing pressures. Four problems encountered by Eanes during his first term of office illustrate this point.

First, reestablishing military hierarchy meant confronting the conservative bias characteristic of the senior military, men in active service on the eve of the revolution who were sidelined during its radicalization but who moved back into positions of responsibility after the 25th of November. In working with others to reestablish a chain of command, Eanes could not easily override their opposition in April 1978 to his own candidate for vice chief of the EMGFA: Lieutenant Colonel Loureiro dos Santos. If professional standards were to be established and given meaning, such an appointment required consultation with the army, navy, and air force heads serving on the General Staff of the Armed Forces. Despite his commitment to modernization of the armed forces, the issue at stake with them at that time was the need to approve Loureiro dos Santos' promotion to four-star general in order to assume the position under discussion. Against the backdrop of dissatisfaction with Caetano's earlier blanketing in of draftees who had served in the field as non-commissioned officers in 1973 and the subsequent purges of the senior military conducted by the captains and majors who had seized power in 1974, Eanes stepped aside, considered the objections of the senior military as legitimate, and accepted Loureiro's resignation. Likewise, Eanes had to give ground again when General Vasco Lourenço, commander of the Lisbon Military Region and a member of the Council of the Revolution, became involved in conflict with the head of the army, General Vasco Rocha Vieira. When conservative military officers demanded Lourenço's resignation, Eanes once again acquiesced, despite his affinity for the moderate left position with which Lourenço was identified and his recognition of the valuable role played by Lourenço in the transition from rule by the radicals to that of the moderates in Portuguese society at large.

Second, modernization of the armed forces meant downgrading the traditional dominance enjoyed by the army, greater resources for the air force, and exacerbation of the rivalry that had existed before the revolution among the different branches, especially that between the army and the navy. Upgrading the air force coincided with demands from within that sector for increased autonomy, yet served to flag for many the fact that one could not assume that these new arrangements and the appointment of new officers would automatically lead to military compliance with actions seen as a threat to the institutional interests of the individual services. Air Force Chief General Lemos Ferreira did not hesitate the least, when faced with substantial cuts by the Assembly of the Republic in 1979, in attacking civilian politicians for rejecting the budget and in suspending on his own air force participation in NATO military exercises without informing the General Staff beforehand. Normalization of military affairs to the contrary, Eanes' position as head of the EMGFA did not mean automatic compliance with his authority in 1979, despite his reinforcement of military hierarchy and work to separate military and civilian affairs.

Third, despite imperfect control over the military institution, Eanes was not dissuaded in the least from his primary goals: enhancement of the authority of the office of president and the constitution of a political movement left of center with an identity distinct from that of the Socialists and the Communists. If that meant giving in to preferences of the military hierarchy in matters deemed important by them in internal military affairs, it strengthened his hand in moving toward his agenda of depoliticizing the military and constituting a political movement that would recapture the reformist aspirations originally expressed by those who identified themselves with social democratic aspirations in the Armed Forces Movement (MFA). Hence, while he dealt with the Council of the Revolution in accord with the legal prescriptions of the Constitution, he made it quite clear that he considered its opinions to be advisory and that he would not be bound by its recommendations. On one critical occasion, when the Council recommended against dismissing Mário Soares as prime minister, he proceeded to do so independently, on the grounds of insufficient support within the Assembly of the Republic for Soares to continue as parliamentary head of government. Likewise, when it came to seeking advice, he preferred to take counsel with his own personal staff in the civilian and military households (*casas civil e militar*) within the Presidency of the Republic.

Fourth, and most importantly, parallel developments in civilian politics converged with changes underway in the military. Francisco Sá Carneiro's election in December 1979 and the formation of the Democratic Alliance by the PSD and CDS parties opened the way for a new accommodation between civilian and military leaders. Despite very different political goals, Sá Carneiro was as interested as Eanes in separating military and civilian affairs. As leader of a center-right alliance, Sá Carneiro was determined to rid Portugal of the excesses of the revolution and to remove from politics those officers identified with the revolution. Despite his later endorsement of a conservative military candidate, General Soares Carneiro, to offset Eanes' reelection bid in the fall of 1980, Sá Carneiro pushed for the formation of a civilian cabinet. The outcome of this initiative was the appointment of a cabinet in January 1980 with civilian ministers of defense and interior. As Bruneau and Macleod point out, this was to be the first time since 1926 that Portugal was to have a cabinet without a single military representative.[6]

Seen in historical context, this move toward exclusively civilian representation within the cabinets serving under the prime minister, coupled with the separation of military and civilian affairs, constituted a significant step in the transition from subjective to objective civilian controls over the military. Yet, at the time, the subsequent battle between Eanes and Sá Carneiro and their respective supporters for control of the presidency obscured the significance of this outcome.

Before 1980 was over the Democratic Alliance had won the elections for the Assembly of the Republic and Sá Carneiro was to be reconfirmed as prime minister, only to die in a tragic airplane accident a short time later in the midst of the presidential campaign. Shortly thereafter Eanes was elected for a second term of office with a substantial margin. Summed up, what all this meant was that, despite the tragedy of Sá Carneiro's death, his emphasis as prime minister on establishing exclusive civilian participation in the cabinet and Eanes' determination to get the military out of politics converged in opening the way for a new era in civil-military relations.

The Breakthrough into a Civilian Controlled Military

My own reading of the events of late 1980 and early 1981 differs from what I would call the conventional wisdom projected by most commentators on the Portuguese scene (be they journalists or academics): Their image conveys the withdrawal of the military from politics between 1976 and 1986 essentially as the consequence of the action of civilian politicians.[7] There is no doubt that the actions of civilians to the center and the right, within the Socialist, PSD, and CDS parties, were an important part of the change in civil-military relations; furthermore, after 1986 they would have the upper hand. But, what needs to be established for comparative purposes in understanding the transitions in the Southern Cone of South America, East-Central Europe, and the Balkans, is that the actions of major military actors—especially General Eanes—were of equal importance. Since summary accounts of party-based action centered in the legislature are available, what would most help in assessing the implications of changes in Portugal's civil-military relations for comparative work would be attention as well to changes in the military institution and the choices made by key military officers involved in questions of public policy.

Just as Huntington's distinction between subjective and objective military controls provides an analytic framework within which to assess changing civil-military relations in Portugal comparatively, so too his distinction among three types of executive civil-military relations organizationally is of relevance in explaining what has been occurring, especially in the transition from Eanes' first to his second administration. Huntington argues that in the evolution of U.S. civil-military relations, the structuring of authority among president, secretary of defense, and military chief reflects a crucial part of the dynamic underway. He sees three patterns as having been present in the American constitutional system as it has evolved. In the "balanced pattern," the president and the secretary play purely political roles, while the head of the military organization is a professional officer and civilian and military officials are used interchangeably to staff non-military operations (such as supply, logistics, and financial management). Under the "coordinate scheme" military and administrative responsibilities immediately below the president are separated. The senior military official is directly accountable to the president for military affairs and serves as the co-equal of the secretary, who is charged with non-military administrative duties. Under such a model, Huntington points out, the military chief must by necessity make political decisions. The "vertical pattern," the third variant, establishes a hierarchical chain of command extending downward from president as commander-in-chief, to secretary, to professional military chief, and to the heads of administrative bureaus and the military services.[8]

No sooner had Eanes won the election than signals were forthcoming from his office, the Presidency of the Republic, that changes in the military command could be expected.[9] Such alterations were to take place in an environment in which it was understood by civilian and military authorities alike that the minister of defense would continue to be a civilian. The model Eanes opted for organizationally was the coordinate scheme. In naming Gen. Melo Egídio to head the EMGFA, the Presidency released detailed information on how these matters were to be handled administratively.[10] Up until this point Eanes had occupied this position himself. In naming Melo Egídio to the post, he sent a clear message that henceforth his role as president would be that of a civilian commander-in-chief and that the ranking military official, the CEMGFA, would have directly under his authority the heads of each of the three major components of the armed forces: Adm. Sousa Leitão as head of navy, Gen. Lemos Ferreira as head of air force, and Gen. Garcia dos Santos as head of army. The previous month Eanes had already prepared for these larger organizational changes by reorganizing his Executive Office, the Casas Civil e Militar, in the direction of bringing together the kind of staff who could offer him the independent advice on political and administrative matters he wished to have.[11]

In his analysis of U.S. experience with the coordinate model Huntington observes that such a model encourages the president to intervene in military affairs and the military chief to make political decisions. This is precisely what transpired in Portugal during these years, although it should be pointed out that in the highly politicized environment prevailing the intermingling of civilian and military affairs in policy questions and in the on-going political debate was unavoidable. The need here, however, is not so much to marshall evidence supporting this interpretation as it is to call attention to where the country stood by the end of Eanes' second term.

Two developments were to become clear. First, political conflict between Eanes as president and the party leadership in parliament resulted in a second settlement in which objective civilian control over the military became the modus operandi. In turning over the presidency to Soares in 1986, the transfer of power took place in an environment reinforcing the role of a civilian president as commander-in-chief of the Portuguese Armed Forces and that of the prime minister as the primary actor designating the minister and secretary of state for national defense. Second, in working out an accommodation with civilian political leaders in parliament, Eanes moved military leaders to the sidelines of the political arena and supported the practice of naming all-civilian cabinets (*Governos*).   He also continued work to develop a coordinate organizational scheme as the appropriate mechanism through which to manage civil-military affairs. Unable politically to retain control over designating the defense minister, he had no choice but to acquiesce to the fact that as the role of civilian government increased, civilian control of the military would have to pass from presidential hands to parliamentary leadership in the Assembly of the Republic, the prime minister and the cabinet official selected by him to oversee military affairs: the defense minister.

Against a background in which civilian and military leaders would continue to spar with each other during these years—with military men criticizing civilian corruption and civilian politicians attacking the military for inappropriate intrusions into politics—the major changes in civil-military relations between 1981 and 1986 were the abolition of the Council of the Revolution, in the context of the constitutional revisions of August 1982, and the adoption of a new law on national defense, that same year. By late 1982, it was apparent another landmark had been established in building a democratic regime, with the Council of the Revolution going out of existence on October 30 and the new defense law entering into effect the next month.

During its existence, the Council of the Revolution remained a source of continual irritation for the center and the right, given its power to declare laws passed by the Assembly of the Republic unconstitutional. From 1976 until 1982 it was the primary source of opposition to undoing the extremes of the revolution, especially any attempt to mitigate the nationalization of the banks and the insurance industry in Portugal. In that regard, while Eanes' position was different from that of the parliamentary leadership, both agreed on the desirability of phasing out the Council of the Revolution.

A new national defense law represented the next step in institutionalizing a democratic regime and redefining civil-military relations. In effect, this round of changes brought to closure a second political "settlement" in post 1974 Portugal. Its basic parameters were: (1) the president's role as commander-in-chief of the armed forces would become largely titular; (2) the senior governmental official managing the day-to-day affairs of the armed forces would be the defense minister; and (3) the selection of the head of the General Staff of the Armed Forces as well as the heads of each of the three armed services would be made not by the president (as Eanes wished) but by the Government (the prime minister and his cabinet). The procedure agreed upon involved selection of the candidates for vacancies in these offices by the Council of the EMGFA, agreement on the candidate by the prime minister and the defense minister, confirmation of the final selection by the Government, and ratification by the president with the understanding that the latter had the power only to accept or reject the selection made. In the event of a rejection of a recommendation by the president, the process would begin over again and continue until prime minister and president were in agreement. Likewise, it was agreed that the parliamentary Government would make the basic decisions on dismissals, with the president being free only to accept or reject its recommendations.

Essentially the work of the PSD-CDS alliance in cooperation with the Socialists (PS), the legislation that became the new defense law was the result of party action in the Assembly of the Republic. Despite Eanes' opposition, the parliamentary leadership pushed through this legislation. When Eanes vetoed it, he found his veto overridden by majority vote on November 26, 1982, and had no choice but to promulgate it as law.

Assertion of the Government's ability to give the new defense law meaning followed immediately with its decision to call for Garcia dos Santos' dismissal as head of the army on July 21, 1983. Despite Eanes' attempt to avoid having to act on the Government's request, it was ultimately a case whereby the cabinet stuck to its authority to make such choices. For, under the terms of the new defense law, the body in which such decisions would be made was the Council for National Defense where the Government in power would have a majority of the votes. The particular form through which this assertion of civilian authority occurred was the vote in this Council rejecting Gen. Garcia dos Santos' recommendation of Gen. Aurélio Trindade as Commander of the Military Region of the North, an action which blocked the normal functioning of the army and placed Garcia dos Santos in a position where he could no longer carry out his military responsibilities effectively.

In the compromise worked out between Prime Minister Soares and President Eanes, after considerable sparring between the two over how the new law was to be interpreted, two agreements were reached. First, from this point forward members of the General Staff would only serve in the event they had the confidence of the Government and the President. Second, in discussing recommendations regarding the naming of new officials or in pressing for dismissals, the principle of reciprocity between president and prime minister would be respected. The fact that this next step in achieving a new settlement over civil-military relations would hold was not clear, however, until three months later. In contrast to the controversy over the Garcia dos Santos dismissal, the replacement at that time of Gen. Melo Egídio as CEMGFA (because he had reached mandatory retirement age) by Air Force Gen. Lemos Ferreira took place without controversy.[12]

This de facto accord represented abandonment of further experimentation with the "coordinate model" favored by Eanes and movement toward a "balanced pattern" of managing civil-military relations, reflective of presidential-parliamentary accommodations. This proved to be much more compatible with the semi-presidential system that had evolved, in which the prime minister and the ranking civilian official, in this case the defense minister, would have jurisdiction over day-to-day affairs in the military institution. In accordance with these new lines of authority, what occurred was restriction of the role of the president in military affairs, by limiting him to responsibilities as commander-in-chief under whose authority was to be found the senior military official, the CEMGFA. Direct presidential authority thus would extend only to questions of policy and deployment of the armed forces in a time of national emergency; all other actions would require working through the legislature. Since the parliamentary Government (the prime minister and his cabinet) controlled the purse strings and already had established the fact that they would select the ranking military officials with the concurrence of the president, they were by definition more centrally involved in all other questions of military policy.

While Balsemão was prime minister (he was Sá Carneiro's successor) and the parliamentary Government weak because of intense party factionalism in the Assembly of the Republic, Eanes was able to continue to exercise major influence and a coordinate system of sorts could still function. But, beginning with the April 1983 elections in which the Socialist party obtained a plurality and subsequently with the formation of the Bloco Central (the Central Bloc), the coalition government of the Socialists and the PSD, the weight of authority began to shift more and more toward the parliamentary Government and away from the Presidency. Despite the fragility of the Bloco Central, it was to last for the full legislative term of four years. In that context, with Soares as prime minister, the significance of civilian control over the military through parliamentary based government was symbolized by the designation of Mota Pinto (PSD) as deputy prime minister and minister of defense (a practice which continued down to 1991). This particular Government continued in power until June 1985. At that point, when the Government fell, Eanes dissolved the Assembly of the Republic and issued a call for new parliamentary elections in October. In the interim, Cavaco Silva emerged as the new head of the PSD; under his leadership the PSD won a plurality and Cavaco Silva was called upon by Eanes to form a caretaker government that would carry over until presidential elections could determine in early 1986 who Eanes' successor would be.

In the highly politicized environment that characterized Portugal during this period, military candidates for public office continued to appear at the behest of civilian politicians. For example, in February 1985, Mota Pinto designated General Firmino Miguel, the deputy chief of staff of the army who had served as Spínola's minister of defense during the first provisional government after 1974, as his presidential candidate. But that nomination met with considerable opposition within the PSD and as a consequence Firmino Miguel later withdrew his name from consideration. Another example would be Eanes' initial choice for president (since he was ineligible for a third term of office under the terms of the Constitution): Colonel Manuel de Costa Bras, the head of the High Authority Against Corruption, who was identified with the moderate left. Yet, he too was not to emerge ultimately as the candidate of the president's party, the PRD, given the opposition expressed to his candidacy from within the party. Like Firmino Miguel, he too was to withdraw his name subsequently.

Once presidential elections were at hand and internal party dynamics had played themselves out, the final list contained only civilian candidates—Diogo Freitas do Amaral, Mário Soares, Francisco Salgado Zenha, and Maria de Lourdes Pintasilgo. From this point forward the major political actors were to be only civilians. Although Freitas won a plurality in the January elections, in the second round in February during which he was pitted against Soares, Soares was the victor. Once installed as president, Soares reaffirmed Cavaco Silva as prime minister. Lacking an absolute majority, Cavaco Silva governed with the support of the opposition, the PRD in particular. Ultimately that arrangement too proved unworkable and Soares dissolved the Assembly of the Republic in April 1987 and called for new parliamentary elections in July; those elections were carried by the PSD under Cavaco Silva's leadership and produced the first absolute majority in the Assembly.

During this period a military presence in politics grew less and less important. The visibility given to the dispute over the selection of General Rocha Vieira as minister of the republic for the Azores by the Cavaco Silva government, despite the protests of Mota Amaral (the regional president of the Azores and a fellow party member), should not deflect attention from these wider, institutional developments. Very clearly, this was an era during which civilian control of politics, with little or no military participation, became accepted practice. With Soares in the presidency and the parliamentary Government in effect setting policy, civil-military relations underwent a final set of changes as a consequence not of decision or settlement but through the de facto political relations that had developed. With Soares taking little or no direct interest in military policy, it was in effect the prime minister and the deputy prime minister, who was also the defense minister, that were in closest contact with the military institution by the end of the decade.

In structural terms, what this has meant is that the pattern of authority dominant since 1987 has now become vertical, with effective political control being exercised by the minister of defense. So far removed from questions of military policy had Soares become by 1987 that, in an anecdotal account published in the Lisbon weekly *Expresso* in February 1987, it was related that—unaware of his prerogative as commander-in-chief to exercise voice in the selection of ranking military officials—he signed off automatically on a recommendation made by the head of the General Staff of the Armed Forces without realizing the significance of his action. Moments later, so the account in the paper went, when an aide questioned the wisdom of this action and he realized what he had done, he went running down the stairs out to the car of the official then departing from the presidential palace to tear up the approval that he had just signed, in order to gain time to review the matter more fully.[13]

Conclusions

While none of these developments represents an end to the contentiousness of civil-military relations, the structural constraints built into the new regime through formal agreements and evolving political relationships have brought about basic change in civil-military affairs. At the same time, one should not conclude that these accords and settlements between the new civilian and military elites extend automatically to the broader society. On the contrary, what they reflect is the separation between the affairs of state and those outside where another dynamic has been going on which must be taken into account as a distinct level of activity. The political settlements discussed above belong essentially in the realm of governance, to the new elites now dominant in Portuguese society. Outside the state in society, at the level of citizens en masse, issues identified with the radical phase of the revolution and the military in politics are very much alive and have become a part of that oral tradition long identified in Portugal with popular culture and those excluded from power. For these people the essence of the revolution and its defeat lies in the mobilization of popular power, coupled with the failure of political leaders on the left to give coherent organizational form to workers' and neighborhood commissions.[14]

Symbolizing the intense emotions and militant political stances that the April 25th movement continues to evoke at the mass level throughout this period are two developments. First, across these years officers and enlisted men identified with the April 25th movement continued to meet and organize themselves politically. The consequence of these activities was the creation of the April 25th Association in late 1983 by officers identified with the April coup, to defend the ideas of the revolution. The other has been the public controversy surrounding Otelo Saraiva de

Carvalho's identification with left-wing extremists, his capture along with militants in the M-25 group in 1980, his subsequent trial, and later imprisonment.

The delay in bringing Otelo and those seized with him to trial, the long and drawn out legal proceedings, their subsequent sentencing, and the debate since over whether or not they should be pardoned in 1987 all point to tremendous sensitivities. Supporting Otelo was a left that perceived itself to be isolated and besieged. Favoring his sentencing was a right who feared that to relax the controls established over such activities would invite a new round of political agitation and radical mobilization.[15]

Still, the peaceful transfer of power from Eanes to Soares in 1986, as Portugal's first civilian president in 60 years, and the PSD's position as the first party to win and maintain an absolute majority since July 1987 signal enormous changes. A new arrangement for handling civil-military relations is in place that does provide, for the first time, effective civilian control over the military. This was exercised first through the Presidency of the Republic and transferred later to the parliamentary Government. Complementing these accords are structural arrangements whereby—beginning with a coordinate structure—a balanced pattern of relationships was established during the Balsemão era and maintained by the sharing of executive authority between president and prime minister until, in the transfer of responsibility to the parliamentary Government, a vertical pattern of authority emerged.

Internally, the armed forces likewise have undergone significant change. Portugal today has a small peace-time army commensurate with its small size and its need to focus on economic modernization. The traditional hegemony of the army over the other two services has also been readjusted in favor of increased autonomy and resources for the air force and the navy, and modernization of the services through integration into the NATO alliance is well underway. At the same time, there is considerable debate over the adequacy of the assistance received to date and the actual extent to which the traditional dominance of the army in military affairs has really been downgraded.

None of this is intended to imply, however, that difficulties and adjustments in civil-military relations are over or that Portugal has moved in the direction of a no-conflict society. What is certain is that as new political issues affecting military interests are forthcoming—for example, grievances over pay—they are more likely than ever to take the form of political representation, in accord with interest group politics as we know them in other democratic societies. The April 25th Association is one such example of the way in which groups of individuals outside the state can constitute themselves for specific purposes and redirect attention to lobbying and public education.

Objective civilian controls, structures promoting vertical executive civil-military relations, and a new professionalism (based not so much on subjective norms transferred through military education and training in staff colleges as on effective participation in a multinational, operationally oriented alliance system) have come into existence. These institutional constraints, coupled with the pressures on Portuguese officers to catch up with their European and American military counterparts, have all converged to create a new set of incentives and inducements. In this setting it is in the best interest of all principal players to enhance the authority of civilian government and to promote the further professionalization and modernization of the Portuguese armed forces.

Nevertheless, one should realize that none of this really has been institutionalized. For more than ten years after the passing of a national defense law (1982), the Ministry of Defense remained little more than an office housing a governmental official with cabinet rank and a secretary of state at the next level, paralleling executive appointments in the rest of the administrative system. The arrangements arrived at have been based on personal understandings among current political leaders. Aside from a flurry of new legislation in early 1993 and a recent effort to staff intermediate positions in the Defense Ministry, there have been few signs of institutional development and concrete interest in effective management of civil-military affairs, as is the case in the development of defense ministries in other democratic governments.

However, it should be recognized that, insofar as external assistance is concerned, the United States has responded to the Portuguese government's request for military support funds to the extent possible. For example, while there was a notable reduction in the level of support received during fiscal year (FY) 1988 and the Portuguese premier made specific reference to the failure of U.S. support to materialize at the levels expected, what Table 3.1 records is a substantial overall increase in the funds set aside for Portugal since 1983.[16] At the same time, from a high of 208 million in security assistance in 1985, support did decline to 117.1 million in 1988.

Compared with Spain, and the level of support given to Portugal in 1983 and before, Portugal has improved its overall position. Furthermore, when the trend in Congress to earmark more and more of the total U.S. foreign assistance package is taken into account, what should be kept in mind is that, as the percentage of money available for discretionary purposes has dropped, the percentage of these moneys allotted to Portugal has increased (see Figure 3.1). For example, once all corrections and adjustments had been made in determining the level of support for FY 89, Portugal ended up with $100 million being set aside in grants; 2.6 million in IMET funds; and 50 million in economic support funds. All told, this came to 152.6 million.

When these various perspectives are summed up, what they reflect is the considerable progress made during the 1980s in establishing two distinct domains, one belonging to professional politicians and the other to the professional military. This record is impressive, particularly when it is compared with the record in the states in Latin America, past and present. The new consensus is one in which the current civilian and military leadership agrees that the affairs of the state are best left to civilians and the conduct of war and national defense, to the military. This outcome, which is the result of internal dynamics in Portuguese society, politics, and governance, is one that warrants greater recognition than has been the case until now and more careful consideration as the merits of increasing, maintaining at current levels, or decreasing U.S. military assistance abroad come under greater scrutiny in a time of economic constraints and pressures to reduce federal deficits.

Should the adjustments made in external assistance in 1989 continue in the future, it may well be that resource scarcity—a problem constant in much of nineteenth and twentieth century Portugal—will be sufficiently reduced so as to facilitate consolidation of these new arrangements. If so, then hopefully this will permit Portuguese leaders to focus on the internal need to build a modern defense ministry with sufficient staff to give administrative content to policies legislated by the Government in national defense and security policy. Should all this occur, a revival of military dissatisfaction with civilian leadership, in the way in which internal military difficulties in the past ultimately have undercut earlier accords in civil-military affairs, may well be neutralized and permit sufficient institutional development to ensure survival of Portugal's new democracy.[17]

Because these considerations involve some very delicate internal questions, they require separate treatment and discussion. Before entering this policy domain, however, it is important to keep in mind that one of the lessons to be learned from such inquiry is the nature of the relationship between democratic transitions and consolidation in key policy arenas. Assessment of these developments and the prospects for institutionalizing Portugal's current practices in civil-military relations within a democratic framework are the concerns of the next two chapters.[18]

TABLE 3.1 U.S. Security Assistance to Countries with American Bases
(in millions of dollars)

	Fiscal Year								
	1980	1981	1982	1983	1984	1985	1986	1987	1988
Turkey	406.3	452.8	702.5	687.8	856.8	878.6	738.0	593.5	525.3
Greece	147.6	178.0	281.2	281.3	501.4	501.4	431.9	344.2	344.4
Spain	132.9	133.2	149.0	414.1	415.0	414.9	396.7	113.0	5.4
Portugal	71.9	77.8	87.4	112.0	147.9	207.5	189.3	147.4	117.1
(ESF	40.0	25.0	20.0	20.0	40.0	80.0	77.0	64.8	32.0)
(MAP	30.0	51.0	20.0	37.5	60.0	70.0	67.0	80.0	80.0)
(IMET	1.9	1.8	2.4	2.0	2.9	2.5	2.3	2.6	2.6)
(FMSC	0	0	45.0	52.5	45.0	55.0	43.1	0	2.5)
Phillippines	9.5	105.6	101.0	101.4	101.5	187.2	324.7	402.6	301.6

Sources: "Shrinking Power: Network of U.S. Bases Overseas Is Unraveling as Need for It Grows," *Wall Street Journal* (WSJ), 29 December 1987, p. 5, and U.S. Department of State, Bureau of Public Affairs, Office of Public Communication, *Background Notes: Portugal* (November 1987).[19]

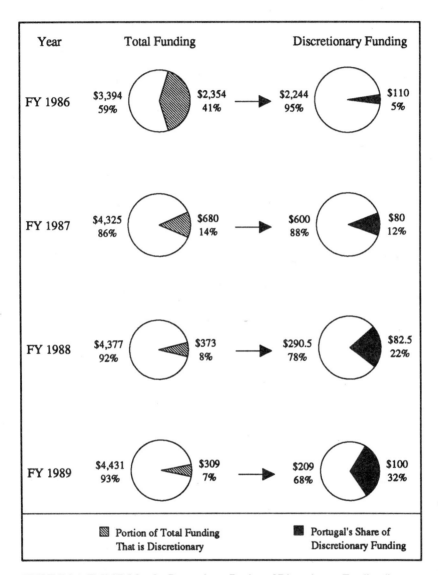

FIGURE 3.1 FMSCR/Map for Portugal as a Portion of Discretionary Funding (in millions of dollars). *Source:* Office of the Secretary of Defense (Washington DC, 1989).

Notes

1. An excellent summation of these patterns in East-Central Europe is to be found in Zoltan Barany, "Regional Disparities and Civil-Military Relations: East-Central and Southeastern Europe," in Lawrence S. Graham (ed.), "Political and Economic Transitions in Eastern Europe and Latin America" (unpublished book manuscript).

2. The key source in this analysis of the military institution in Brazil, both in its role in the Brazilian transition and in pointing out how it has given up none of its military prerogatives, is Alfred Stepan, *Rethinking Military Politics: Brazil and the Southern Cone* (Princeton, NJ: Princeton University Press, 1988),

3. This distinction between subjective and objective civilian controls over the military is based on distinctions drawn by Samuel P. Huntington in *The Soldier and the State: The Theory and Politics of Civil-Military Relations* (Cambridge: Harvard University Press, 1957). It builds on the application of these ideas to the Portuguese case, as developed by Thomas C. Bruneau and Alex Macleod at the end of chapter 1 in their book *Politics in Contemporary Portugal: Parties and the Consolidation of Democracy* (Boulder, CO: Lynne Rienner Publishers, 1986). "Subjective" controls are those used by a particular civilian group or groups to influence the military, or a section of it, to further its own power aims. "Objective" civilian controls entail treatment of the military as a professional body by civilian authorities, recognition of their separate spheres of professional competence, and use of the military as the "tool of the state" (in the sense that its role in society is determined and established by civilian authorities and rendered neutral politically). See in particular Hungtington's discussion of these points pp. 80-86 and the use made of these concepts, as a way of explaining changes in the Portuguese military during the early 1980s, by Bruneau and Macleod on p. 24.

4. This label—used in the previous chapter to distinguish an ill-defined center in the military institution from the extremes on the right and the left—is intended to identify those officers caught in the middle, be they slightly to the left and hence favorable to democratic socialism or slightly to the right and identified with a social democratic perspective.

5. A succinct characterization of this group of military officers is to be found in "Armed Forces: 'Silent Majority' Commands," in the special supplement published on Portugal in the *International Herald Tribune*, 3 June 1981, p. 14S.

6. Bruneau and Macleod, p. 15.

7. The most explicit statement of this perspective is to be found in Bruneau and Macleod, *Politics in Contemporary Portugal*. See especially chapter 1 "The Military: Goodbye to Politics?" and the conclusion and epilogue to their book. Less explicit but no less wedded to the premise of the primacy of parties after 1976, with little regard for political dynamics within the military institution, is Walter Opello's *Portugal's Political Development: A Comparative Approach* (Boulder, CO: Westview Press. 1985).

8. These organizational dimensions of civil-military relations are based on Huntington's discussion of "The Structural Constant" in chapter 8, especially pp. 186-89, in *The Soldier and the State*. By using Huntington's constructs and building on his work, which is essentially a study of how civil-military relations evolved in the U.S. context and strengthened commitment to a democratic system, I wish to return to the interplay between personality and organization in structuring civil-military relations in democratic society, comparatively. If one considers the post-civil-war era as formative in the evolution of mass democracy in the United States, then likewise the direction General William T. Sherman took the U.S. military and the subsequent evolution in U.S. civil-military relations becomes as much a part of the kind of state that was being created as the United States emerged as a world power, as anything going on in the economic sphere vis-a-vis Congress, the parties, the federal civilian bureaucracy, and the business community.

9. "Eanes prepara mudanças nas chefias militares," *Expresso*, 20 December 1980, p. 10.

10. This information was summarized by Miguel Almeida Fernandes, with a supporting organizational chart of the military component of the coordinate scheme, in "A reestruturação nas Forças Armadas: Estudo de psicólogos indica Melo Egídio como o homem certo para CEMGFA," *Expresso*, 21 February 1981, p. 3.

11. "Eanes remodela as suas Casas Civil e Militar," *Expresso*, 10 January 1981, p. 1.

12. For greater detail on these developments in the assertion of the Government's authority over the military in 1982 and 1983, see the discussion in Bruneau and Macleod, pp. 16-20.

13. See the account of this incident in *Expresso*, "Uma substituição militar," in the section "Gente a solta," 14 February 1987, p. 11.

14. The book that best captures the popular power mobilized during the revolution and this distinctive thrust to the Portuguese transition from dictatorship to democracy is: John L. Hammond, *Building Popular Power: Workers' and Neighborhood Movements in the Portuguese Revolution* (New York: Monthly Review Press, 1988).

15. See the account by Jane Kramer of Otelo Saraiva de Carvalho's imprisonment and trial, "Letter from Europe (Otelo Nuno Romano Saraiva de Carvalho and the Portuguese Revolution)," *The New Yorker*, 63:11 (November 30, 1987), p. 105 ff., as well as the various news stories on this topic in *Expresso* published over the years, especially 11 April 1987, p. 5; 30 May 1987, p. 34R ff.(in the magazine supplement); and 31 October 1987, p. 5.

16. This particular point was touched on in Cavaco Silva's remarks following his discussions with President Reagan in February 1988. He made a particular point of expressing his government's disappointment in their failure to receive the military assistance expected "particularly at a time when we are committed to the reequipment of our armed forces and trying to modernize the country in an effort that cannot be deferred." *Weekly Compilation of Presidential Documents*, Monday February 29, 1988, vol. 24, no. 8, p. 251.

17. For helpful comments made on initial drafts of this chapter, I am indebted to Kenneth Maxwell, Thomas Bruneau, Rafael Bañón Martínez, and Judith Cefkin. For a useful and informative account of the role of the armed forces in Portuguese politics before 1976, see Maria Carrilho, *Forças Armadas e Mudança Política em Portugal no. Sec. XX: Para uma Explicação Sociológica do Papel dos Militares* (Lisbon: Estudos Gerais, Série Universitária, Imprensa Nacional—Casa da Moeda, 1985). For a comparative statement of the historic problem presented by military involvement in politics in Latin America and the difficulty of obtaining a redefinition of civil-military relations in order to consolidate democratic regimes, see: Alain Rouquié, *The Military and the State in Latin America*, trans. Paul E. Sigmund (Berkeley and Los Angeles: University of California Press, 1987).

18. This chapter and the first part of the next contain revised material from an earlier publication, entitled "The Military: Modernization and Changing Perspectives," which I published in *Portugal Defense and Foreign Policy since Democratization*, ed. Kenneth Maxwell (New York: Camões Center Special Report No. 3, Research Institute on International Change, Columbia University, 1991), pp. 14-28. The tables published there are reproduced here in their entirety.

19. Since the figures published in the WSJ reflect numerous inaccuracies and do not match actual appropriations, they have been adjusted according to the *Congressional Presentation for Security Assistance Programs, Fiscal Year 1989* (Washington, DC: U.S. Government Printing Office, 1988), pp. 167, 291, 295, 327, 361, as well as to budgetary information available for previous fiscal years. Budgetary allocations list four categories of programs: Economic Support Funds (ESF), Military Assistance Program (MAP), International Military Education and Training Program (IMET), and Foreign Military Sales Credit Program (FMSC). Because these funding categories do not match the subcategories used in the WSJ article, the above table has also been corrected by listing these four programs as actually funded. In addition, adjustments in the total figures given for Turkey, Greece, Spain, and the Philippines in the WSJ have also been made in light of actual allocations. The reader should be aware of the fact that the greatest discrepancies in the WSJ article occur in their listing of much higher totals for the Philippines than was actually the case for the years 1980 through 1986.

4

Problems Encountered in Assigning the Military a New Mission in a Consolidated Democracy

As the two previous chapters have demonstrated, Portugal's civil-military relations have undergone tremendous changes over the last two decades. These alterations constitute an integral part of Portugal's successful transition to democracy. Whereas the 1970s involved a major reorientation in mission, the 1980s were marked by the subordination of the military to civilian authority. These adjustments required major modifications in the military institution.

The shift from mass-conscription armed forces, organized to fight guerrilla movements in Africa, to a small peacetime army and an expanded navy and air force, focused on the North Atlantic and Portugal's NATO commitment, was largely in place by the end of the 1980s. With military hierarchy restored and a clear-cut separation of civil and military affairs in place, civilian and military authorities have been able to turn their attention to building a new set of relationships.

Changes Within the Military Institution as a Consequence of Its New Role

The impact of these changes on the military can best be seen by referring to two sets of figures: those on the size of the armed forces (in absolute numbers as well as a percentage of the labor force) and those on military expenditures as a percentage of GDP. As can be seen by examining Table 4.1, if in 1974, on the eve of the revolution, Portugal reported

282,000 men in arms, in 1980 the total size of the armed forces was 83,000. While comparable figures are not available in standard sources for the next five years, those given for 1986 suggest an even greater reduction: 63,500 (of whom 39,000 were in the army, 15,000 in the navy, and 9,500 in the air force).[1] Seen as a percentage of the total labor force, Table 4.2 records a decline from a high of 8.0 percent of the labor force serving in the armed forces in 1973, to 2.2 percent for the years 1978 through 1980. In terms of defense expenditures as a percentage of GDP, from a high of 7.4 percent in 1974, Portugal reported but 3.6 percent in 1980. Compared with the average defense expenditures of the NATO countries as a whole, Table 4.3 shows the following: If in 1970 Portugal was spending 7.0 percent of GDP on its armed forces as opposed to 3.7 percent for NATO as a whole, it had dropped to 3.4 percent for Portugal in 1980 as compared to 3.6 percent for NATO as a whole. Expressed in budgetary terms, defense expenditures declined from an estimated high of 50 percent in 1970 to about 10.2 percent in 1984.[2]

These figures reflect the tremendous readjustments the armed forces have been undergoing. This has consisted of transition from a much larger, extra-continental fighting force, focused on defending Portuguese territory in Africa, to that of a very small contingent officially integrated into NATO, but in practice operating only at its margins.

Despite the continuation of internal differences, most accounts give the impression that the officer corps today is quick to defend the integrity of the military as an institution apart from civil society. The general consensus also seems to be that the officer corps conceives its new role to be that of guarantor of the new regime, rather than a direct participant. This does not rule out the involvement of individual officers in electoral politics, as the previous chapter has shown, but as an institution the armed forces had clearly disengaged themselves from politics by the end of the 1980s. At the same time, despite the redirection of attention to defense of Portugal's Atlantic Triangle, it is probably more realistic to say that, in the absence of sufficient internal resources to match the external supports received in order to thoroughly modernize the armed forces, no concrete way has yet emerged for giving positive content to these new perspectives and hence for operationalizing a new mission for the Portuguese military.

As a consequence, frustration levels are rising. In comparing these sentiments to those articulated historically in the peninsula or in Latin

America under similar conditions, a revival of the military's interest in politics as a way to secure its place in society should not be ruled out. On the one hand, the extensive military support expected from the United States has not materialized to the extent anticipated by the Portuguese, while on the other the Assembly of the Republic has made no real readjustments in salary commensurate with the professionalization alluded to as so desirable for the military institution. At best what the Portuguese press reports is parity with civil servants, although military officers would dispute this in terms of the scales used to equate military and civilian salaries at the managerial level.[3]

Matching discontent with the absence of attention to internal military needs by the civilian leadership is the feeling that politics rather than performance is what really counts in one's career advancement, in the positive as well as the negative sense. Supporting the former would be the discussion centering around General Soares Carneiro's appointment as vice-head of the General Staff (one that was seen in 1987 as a reward for having served the PSD as its candidate for president in 1980 against Eanes). In the latter case, many would cite the censoring of Lieutenant Colonel Vasco Lourenço and his five day jail sentence for his militant stance on celebrating the anniversary of the 25th of April despite instructions from his superiors to desist.[4]

Given the subordination of the military to civilian authority, the unanswered question and challenge for the 1990s concerns whether or not it will be possible, as modernization of the economy proceeds ahead (to meet the demands of full-fledged participation in the European Community), it will be possible also to create a small, modern armed forces capable of operating and performing at a level equal to that of their NATO counterparts. Such a transformation will require not only extensive new equipment but also advanced training and levels of professionalization hitherto unknown in Portugal. In assessing the extent of modernization needed in Portugal in all sectors, once again conjectural factors introduce an element of great uncertainty since it remains to be seen what will be the long-term impact of the opening to the east, due to the collapse of Communist governments in Eastern Europe during 1989 and 1990 and the reallocation of funds hitherto concentrated in Southern Europe to meet growing demands and emergencies in East Central Europe, the territories originally comprising the Soviet Union, and the Balkans.

Unresolved Issues in Civil-Military Relations

Despite all that has been written and said about modernizing Portugal's armed forces, then, it is not at all clear how competing demands and priorities in civil and military affairs are going to be met in the years ahead. Certainly there is no shortage of information and commentary regarding the alternatives open to the country. Likewise, a good deal of agreement has emerged over the appropriateness of the reductions in expenditure and size already in place and the redefinition of mission that has occurred since 1974. Yet to date, little has been accomplished in determining the extent of the reorganization needed, the costs required in further professionalization, and the relationship of these issues to broader questions of public policy. A key aspect in all this will be whether or not the armed forces and the defense community will be able to communicate sufficiently to civilian politicians, especially those identified with the PSD, the need to retain a wider Atlantic relationship instead of the Euro-centric orientation characteristic of the Cavaco Silva government.

In assessing the prospects for success in modernizing the military institution, accomplishments as well as difficulties need to be taken into account. As indicated in the previous chapter, a new national defense law has been on the books since 1982. Formal statements regarding national security and defense policy have since been prepared and sanctioned by the Government in the form of a resolution passed by the Council of Ministers in 1985. After considerable delay, action also is now being taken to give substance and content to the 1987 decree law providing for the organization and staffing of the defense ministry, not as a large ministerial organization patterned after the Spanish example but as a small office capable of exercising budgetary and oversight authority. Consensus within the country's political leadership and the public at large has likewise emerged regarding the importance of continued commitment to NATO, the strategic importance of the Azores and Madeira in European security, and the extent of the autonomy appropriate for these islands.

In contrast, when questions are raised concerning the trade-offs entailed in pursuing one set of priorities as opposed to another in budgetary terms, or when actions are debated that touch upon the interests of one of the major actors, silence ensues. Seen from this perspective, concrete programs and clear-cut commitments implementing goals agreed upon and prescribing concrete activities are singularly lacking. Furthermore, when one attempts to pin down the ability of the Government to exercise effective authority over the military, it seems as though, now that the PSD majority government has established formal political authority, it has been content since to leave open other all questions concerning specifically what modernization of the nation's armed forces really means, until the amount of foreign support in these questions can be determined—given the adjustments which are being made within the United States and Western Europe as a consequence of the Soviet collapse.

Nevertheless, it is important to keep in mind that getting the military to disengage from politics, removing questions of party preferences from internal debates over promotions, and naming military superiors independently of partisan considerations were not easily accomplished. Since such changes required negotiating political accords, the terms of the agreements reached remain relevant today. They constitute factors which explain in large part the slowness with which political and military authorities alike have approached the question of creating an effective defense ministry and reallocating resources within the armed forces in accord with their new mission. To change the status quo means to run the risk of reopening old issues and differences that have divided military and civilian authorities alike.

While the politics inherent in these accomodations are well understood by all the major participants, it is not so clear that the institutional implications of these actions are equally well appreciated. What these settlements entailed was strengthening the role of the General Staff of the Armed Forces (the Estado Maior Geral das Forças Armadas, the EMGFA), at the time civilian and military actors were working toward the extinction of the Council of the Revolution (the Conselho da Revolução, the CR). Once that was accomplished the next task entailed building consensus among political and military leaders over the shape of a new defense law that would regulate civil-military affairs in Portugal's new democracy.

The Impact of the Portuguese Settlement on Military Bureaucracy

The marginalization of the CR in the early 1980s and its eventual abolition in 1982 produced unanticipated institutional consequences that have continued to plague all governments since. While the protracted nature of the political settlements and accomodations reached have had a positive impact in terms of contributing to democratic consolidation, one should not ignore their costs in terms of weakening the capacity of the state subsequently to deal with substantive policy issues. This situation has had as much impact on the military institution as it has had on civilian sectors interested in innovative economic and social policy that will deal substantively with Portugal's historic underdevelopment vis-a-vis its European neighbors.

It is at this point that consideration of the Portuguese state must be interjected as a related but distinct component in understanding the transition to a democratic regime and its consolidation. Whereas the Salazar state was a strong state with considerable capacity not only to implement policy but also to exclude from contestation issues that were troublesome to the regime (namely, the colonial question), the democratic state that has emerged since 1976 is a weak state, subject to considerable penetration by outside interests and pressures. To understand the impact of these developments, first, on civil-military relations and military bureaucracy, and, later, on economic and social policy, it is essential to keep in mind the fact that the consolidation of a democratic regime in Portugal has remained essentially a political endeavor. Furthermore, the conservative thrust of PSD Governments since 1987 has meant that civil-military relations and questions pertaining to military bureaucracy have been handled largely according to the interests of political coalitions and alignments outside the state. The same applies to economic and social policy. The emphasis on economic restructuring, through building a new set of triangular relationships between the Government, the private sector, and the European Community (centered around "Eurocrats" in Brussels), has led both to a bypassing of the state and to an emphasis on economic restructuring, largely devoid of concern with social policy.[5]

Because the Portuguese settlement required first negotiating the exit of the military from politics and later building consensus among the major civilian actors over the rules which would regulate political competition in the new regime, the issue of the kind of state needed in a democratic Portugal has never received the attention it deserves. As a consequence military officials as much as civilian bureaucrats have been constrained by institutions of governance originally designed to secure order and control under authoritarian rule and subsequently modified in a haphazard way to respond to new needs and priorities in what has become a much more open society and economy. In this kind of institutional context in which accountability and responsibility are poorly defined, one cannot deal with the question of civil-military relations in isolation from questions of the state. But, in order to deal with these two issues—civil-military relations in a democratic Portugal and the role of a state (which of necessity must involve social and economic questions distinct from those of concern to the military)—one must keep in mind how persistent the Salazar reforms of the Portuguese state after 1932 and its structuring according to two distinct bureaucratic components, one military and the other civilian, have been.

Under the terms of the old order, only Salazar through his supraministry, the Presidency of the Council of Ministers, had the capacity to control and coordinate the state apparatus. After first tracing the lines of authority within the state during the Caetano era and later attempting to follow the changing patterns of authority during the revolutionary era (1974-1976) and after that during the building of a democratic regime, my own conclusion is that divided authority and compartmentalization within the state was an essential component of the old order, once one moved below the Presidency of the Council. The de facto removal of the cupola, despite the retention of the designation of the Presidency of the Council since, has made it singularly difficult to sort these relationships out.

The disjunctures present in the current situation and yet the continuities between past and present require two distinct lines of analysis. This chapter and the next, consequently, build on and continue the focus on civil-military relations. Once this topic has been brought to closure, attention will then shift to questions of civilian bureaucracy (the focus of chapters six and seven). The difficulty in this line of analysis lies in tackling the challenge of establishing a holistic view of state and society when for the last sixty years the state has been bifircuated into two distinct components—one, military; the other, civilian—and has moved from a position of strength and coherency to one of weakness and dispersion of authority.

Insofar as civil-military relations are concerned, what all this means is that the Portuguese state since 1976 has inherited a military bureaucratic entity in the form an expanded EMGFA which has had responsibilities that in other societies are usually assigned to defense ministries.[6] Largely staffed since the Revolution and housed in the old Overseas Ministry building in Restelo, the EMGFA was filled with officers prepared to make higher levels of decision than was to be the case once civilian rule was consolidated. Given responsibility initially for ensuring the separation of military and civilian affairs and reestablishing control and discipline within the armed forces, the EMGFA ceased to have effective power to implement military policy once the policy-making organ for which it had been intended as its administrative arm (the CR) ceased to exist. The rapidity with which a new civilian-dominated democratic regime emerged meant that political events superseded formal institutional arrangements.

The conflict between President Eanes and the various heads of Government (the prime minister and the defense minister) over whether the new regime was to be essentially presidential or parliamentary-centered was eventually resolved in favor of·the civilian leadership in the Assembly of the Republic.[7] This involved several nuances that shaped the institutional component in civil-military relations subsequently which should be kept in mind. Despite Eanes' designation of a military officer other than himself as armed forces chief at the beginning of his second term of office (in early 1981), he remained in effect their head and the single most important individual in determining the content of military policy and ensuring acquiescence of the armed forces to the assertion of civilian supremacy. Offsetting Eanes' military influence was the consolidation of civilian authority in determining the heads of the EMGFA and the individual services during 1983. This was institutionalized afterwards through the practice of designating the defense minister as the vice prime minister. At the same time, since implementation of national security and defense policy insofar as the armed forces were concerned remained the responsibility of the EMGFA, the EMGFA continued to exercise significant influence in determining day-to-day administrative actions. In effect, it has come to constitute a separate tier of military bureaucrats operating between the defense ministry and the armed services.

The consequences of these outcomes have been twofold. First, a much larger percentage of routine national defense and security policy questions related to military performance—such as redefining the military's mission and determining the content of the cutbacks imposed on the nation's armed forces—have continued to be decided by military personnel assigned to the EMGFA. Elsewhere, once civilian supremacy was established, separately constituted defense ministries with an expanding policy role have emerged and assumed these responsibilities. In the context of democratic transitions in other societies, this can be seen clearest by looking at the Spanish case.

Secondly, and more importantly, the effectiveness of the EMGFA as an organ for coordinating and controlling individual service activities has at the very same time been constrained by the way in which civilian dominance of military affairs has been exercised since 1987. While the individual services have always enjoyed considerable autonomy, what has become a new factor in civil-military relations since this date has been the extent to which the PSD has exercised its own partisan influences, once it was able to assert its own preferences first in having Soares Carneiro designated as vice-head of the EMGFA and later, after it had gained majority power, as EMGFA head. In addition, bypassing the EMGFA, the PSD leadership has preferred to deal with the individual services directly, in determining their heads and setting up channels for direct communication with them. What these actions have done is to revive the earlier practice of opting for subjective political controls, in order to move to the forefront military personnel more in sympathy with the PSD, and to undercut Eanes' earlier initiatives to build a new set of objective controls as a key component in consolidating a democratic regime.

In turn, the way in which the Government has used its power to determine who will head the armed forces has reversed the previous pattern in civil-military relations and produced unexpected consequences in the power relations between president and prime minister. As the Presidency of the Republic came to exercise less and less influence over military affairs after 1982, the Government (acting through the Presidência do Conselho, the Presidency of the Council of Ministers) increased its dominance of such matters. Yet today in the early 1990s a very different situation exists. Whereas Soares assumed office in early 1987 as the first civilian president in over a half century with little real interest in or influence over military affairs, by 1989 his use of the symbolic powers of president as Head of State had given him both stature and respect as Commander-in-Chief of all the nation's armed forces, above and beyond partisan influence. The institutional consequence of these outcomes has been the revival of the Office of the President as an independent power center, detached from the politics of senior military appointments and capable of offsetting more partisan political intiatives coming from the Office of the Prime Minister, and interested in reinforcing objective civilian controls.

Obstacles to the Institutionalization of Civilian Oversight Authority

This institutional setting also explains the differences between design and outcome in implementing Portugal's new defense law. Despite the significance of the defense law as an instrument of political accord in 1982, insofar as the formal structures of government are concerned, this new law has actually exercised little influence over the dispersal of power in questions of national defense and security policy and the shifting patterns of influence over such matters between the Offices of the President and the Prime Minister.[8] In this setting, the interpretation given to this law's implementation in questions regarding internal military affairs has served to strengthen the clout of the staffs of the individual services and has focused attention within them on the criteria to be used in making senior appointments and the rights of enlisted men. The result of these developments has been to marginalize the EMGFA further without reducing its formal standing as an organization superior to the individual services. This has led, in turn, to new bureaucratization within military affairs since as an organ that is frequently bypassed both by the parties and the services, the principal resource the EMGFA has is its control over internal bureaucratic procedures and formal channels of communication between the services and the offices of the minister and secretary of state for defense.

Yet another dimension to be taken into account is the gradualness with which issues related to depoliticizing and displacing the military from active participation in questions of public policy continue to be approached. In this regard, the strategy and procedures followed in drawing up, debating, and arriving at two-third's support in the

Assembly of the Republic for a new national defense law merit comment. Rather than a law imposed by majority vote, a conscious strategy of involvement and participation on the part of all crucial actors—military as well as civilian—took precedence. Not only was broad-based political party agreement established in advance, but the Government's initial draft reflected ample and detailed discussion with the senior military on a point by point basis of the defense law proposed in parliament. The result of these lengthy discussions and debates was a general agreement or settlement regarding the procedures to be followed that has facilitated policy making in other areas. Thus, while many in the senior military were not happy with major components of the law, they accepted it because they viewed it as a legitimate reflection of majority political preferences within Portugal. As a consequence, they cooperated in its promulgation and entering into effect. Equally important was the role played by the President (Eanes), who when he saw his veto overriden, emphasized the correctness and the legitimacy of the procedures through which it had been ratified and sanctioned. Once in place, this new defense law has come to symbolize the civil-military accord reached: civilian supremacy in public affairs.

Once again, earlier outcomes such as these have direct bearing on the present impasse. No one wishes to upset earlier accords. To deal with either—creating an effective civilian-controlled defense ministry, which would further displace the EMGFA, or reallocating resources, which would benefit some and penalize others within the armed forces—carries the threat of repoliticizing military affairs and reopening questions regarding the formal and informal rules regulating the conduct of civil-military relations.

Whereas subordination of the military to civilian authority was essential in the consolidation of the new regime, the advent of majority political power in a single party organization (the PSD) since 1987 and preoccupation with the economic changes necessary to meet the January 1, 1993, deadline of full integration into the European Community have had the effect of marginalizing many questions of a defense and security nature. With questions of economic policy dominant and a relaxation of East-West tensions underway, civil-military relations in the 1990s no longer have the same immediacy for party politicians that they did during the 1980s. In particular, the shift over the last five years in the issues dominating public debate, from military to economic affairs, has taken place to such an extent that the agenda entailed in adopting new concepts of defense and security policy has yet to receive serious consideration in the budgetary decisions and allocations which must be made if they are to be given meaningful content.

This is not to question in the least the priority given to economic modernization and the focusing of attention on the changes necessary in the public and private sectors in order to respond to the challenges ahead. Yet, when the nation's broader policy setting is examined, if economic modernization is to be given a priority and further modernization of the armed forces is to be placed on hold except for equipment and economic support negotiated from abroad, then there are some hard and difficult decisions in military policy to be made that necessitate conscious action rather than decision by default. For, failure to act much longer will in effect impose decisions through inaction in the medium and long-term in national security and defense policy that may well not be in the best interest of either civilian or military leaders in the years ahead. The initial hopes of a new era of peace in Europe with the ending of the Cold War, so prevalent in 1989, have by 1993 given way to new uncertainties in the midst of conflict in the Balkans and Transcaucasia.

In this setting, where the reallocation of economic resources within the armed forces and implementation of the new mission assigned to them has in effect been deferred, it is not entirely inappropriate to consider some of the essential groundwork that needs to be, and can be, laid at this time in relating questions of strategy and the management of scarce resources to military affairs. Elsewhere, when numerous institutional interests have been at stake and major adjustments in priorities have had to be made, the introduction of a policy pespective and concepts of strategic management have facilitated the setting of priorities, the establishment of a hierarchy of needs, and reconsideration of budgetary allocations and the impact of each of these actions on the human resources available.

One of the outcomes of the increasing limitations on public financial resources in the 1980s elsewhere has been the introduction of rationally conceived cutback management procedures, as available public funds have declined and social agendas related to such issues as the environment, public services, health care, and housing have expanded. Properly handled, reductions in public funding for one activity as opposed to another can open up the opportunity for a redefinition of goals and priorities. Such crises need not produce political impasses but can also facilitate new courses of action excluded from consideration as long as one is locked into established bureaucratic procedures, prior institutional priorities that have long been accepted as a given, and outlooks reflecting the interests of individual institutions which have sufficient power to veto new action, but are incapable of moving beyond the limitations of the present.

To date, little effective use has been made in Portugal of the academic community in the social sciences and the application of its perspectives, concepts, and methods to important policy problems and questions. Yet, if one will look back over the development of the social sciences in Portugal since 1974, the quantity and the quality of Portuguese social science research and writing has increased to an extent inconceivable for anyone laboring in these areas during the early 1970s.[9] Elsewhere policy studies, and the subfields of national defense and security policy studies, have served as catalysts for bringing together the resources scattered in a multitude of different public and private organizations—some in civil society; others, within the military institution and in the training and educational units it has developed in the effort to create a more professionalized military. While support for staff colleges and expanded military training in Central and South America during the 1970s served to strengthen the military with pernicious consequences for civil society, such an outcome is not necessarily predetermined. Rather, by approaching national defense and security policy studies more openly, it is equally possible to conceive of them as an essential ingredient in building and maintaining a democratic society and in directing attention to equally great needs in funding and supporting work on the new technologies and the setting of economic priorities.

Certainly one can identify various work groups that have been established and are currently operating in these domains in Portugal. But what is missing, and where there is untapped potential available for constructive work, is basic research. Without a more adequate knowledge base and without making research and writing on questions of national security and defense policy in comparative context academically respectable, it is difficult to conceive how serious progress can be made on what are some very difficult questions and choices which soon will have to be made in Portugal by the Portuguese themselves.

Granted there are those who would argue that a small country such as Portugal really has no place today for much of a military establishment, in light of the democracy achieved and the prospects that lie ahead with European economic integration and growing political ties of a continental nature. Yet perhaps, in considering these perspectives, a review of the nation's own military history in modern times might be of assistance. This is not the first time that civilian reformers have advocated dismantlement of the nation's defense capability and reliance on external alliances as the most effective way to protect Portugal's own national interests. On the eve of the Napoleonic wars of the last century it was assumed that Portugal's alliance system was sufficient to attend to the nation's security and defense needs, in the context of an impoverished state. Subsequently, faced with an external challenge and the departure of the Court for Brazil, military defense was sadly lacking and foreign occupation of Portuguese territory, easily accomplished. Later, in reacting to the consequences that ensued from an invasion that could not be contained, at great cost in terms of human lives and physical infrastructure it was the civilian population north of the Tagus, in cooperation with Portuguese military leadership, that played an indispensable role in reestablishing national integrity in the aftermath of those events.[10]

TABLE 4.1
Size of the Armed Forces
(in thousands)

Year:	70	71	72	73	74	75	76	77	78	79	80
Size:	229	244	260	276	282	104	83	79	82	81	83

Source: The North Atlantic Treaty Organization: Facts and Figures (Brussels: NATO Information Service, 1981), pp. 319, 323.

TABLE 4.2
Armed Forces as Percentage of Total Labor Force

Year:	70	71	72	73	74	75	76	77	78	79	80
% Labor/ Force:	6.5	6.9	7.4	8.0	7.1	2.8	2.2	2.1	2.2	2.2	2.2

Source: The North Atlantic Treaty Organization: Facts and Figures (Brussels: NATO Information Service, 1981), pp. 319, 323.

TABLE 4.3
Defense Expenditures as Percentage of GDP

Year:	70	71	72	73	74	75	76	77	78	79	80
% GDP:	7.0	7.4	6.9	6.0	7.4	5.3	4.0	3.5	3.5	3.5	3.4

Source: The North Atlantic Treaty Organization: Facts and Figures (Brussels: NATO Information Service, 1981), pp. 319, 323.

Notes

1. Source: *Defense and Foreign Affairs Handbook* (Washington, DC: Perth Corp., 1986), pp. 601-2.

2. This 50 percent figure appears in "Portugal Survey," *The Economist*, 28 May 1988, p. 10, and is the one most generally reported in a variety of news sources, although it is difficult to document in official Portuguese sources. The 1984 figure comes from the 1986 *Defense and Foreign Affairs Handbook* (Washington, DC: Perth Corp., 1986), p. 602. Those on NATO as a whole, in terms of defense expenditures as a percentage of GDP, come from *The North Atlantic Treaty Organization: Facts and Figures* (Brussels: NATO Information Service, 1981), p. 319.

3. See, for example, the article "Militares aumentados 11.5%," *Expresso*, 14 February 1987, p. 2.

4. For documentation of these two issues, see "Salgado Zenha: O Governo sofre do optimismo panglóssico do dr. Soares" (interview), *Expresso*, magazine supplement, 14 February 1987, p. 35R, and "Manifestações pro Vasco Lourenço preocupam hierarquia militar," *Expresso*, 13 June 1987, p. 4. For a brief assessment of the military at the end of the decade, see the discussion in "Portugal Survey," *The Economist*, 28 May 1988, p. 10.

5. Generally speaking, an academic literature on this aspect of Portuguese politics, which permits comparison, does not exist. Accompanying the emergence of this new political class, with a strong commitment to political democracy, is an extensive body of political studies, published without and outside Portugal. But, for the most part these studies focus on parties, elections, and the mobilization of mass constituencies—on the inputs into democratic rule. Rare are the instances of studies on the output side, assessing policy outcomes and issues of whether or not these changes in politics have increased the quality of life for the majority. Yet, the importance of assessing accomplishments and failures in economic and social policy can be seen through the eyes of the "informed" press—in such newspapers as the *Financial Times*, the *Herald Tribune*, and the *Christian Science Monitor*. An excellent example of what is to be gained through comparative reflection on the priorities given to economic restructuring versus social policy is to be found in Howard LaFranchi, "Greece, Portugal Test EC Capacity to Grow," *Christian Science Monitor*, 23 July 1992, pp. 6-7.

6. The basic source for understanding military bureaucracy in Portugal is: Ministério da Defesa Nacional (Portugal), *Livro Branco da Defesa Nacional, 1986* (Lisbon: Gabinete do Ministro, Ministério da Defesa Nacional, 1986). In particular see the discussion of the CEMGFA and its organizational chart on pp. 79-81.

7. At this point, to follow this line of reasoning and analysis, it is important to introduce several key operational definitions. This is because in the domain of public sector studies, the basic concepts one must work with concern "state," "government," and "regime." Applied to the Portuguese case, these distinctions become clearer through analogy. Where the old regime was authoritarian, the new one is and remains democratic. That is to say, the structuring of power and power relationships has changed fundamentally through the removal of constraints on participation and the contestation of public issues.

Likewise, government—i.e., the collective set of those public officials occupying presidential and parliamentary leadership roles—today is accountable to the majority through open, competitive elections, whereas prior governments were accountable only to themselves or, when power was vested in the hands of a single man, to the one they served. But the state apparatus—the institutions of governance comprised of ministries, commissions, and quasi-public entities attached to central organs by design or circumstance—continues to be defined largely by the same statutes and norms that have long belonged to a common corpus of public law, and, within that, administrative law.

8. The primary sources discussing the content of this law and the intense politicking which was necessary to get it drawn up and approved is contained in the following works of Diogo Freitas do Amaral: "A Elaboracao da Lei de Defesa Nacional e das Forças Armadas," in *A Feitura das Leis*, vol. 1 (Oeiras: no publisher, 1987), pp. 117-38; "La Constitución y las Fuerzas Armadas," *Revista de Estudios Políticos*, (*Nueva Epoca*), Nums. 60-61 (April-Septiembre 1988), pp. 607-20 (reissued in Portuguese as "A Constituição e as Forças Armadas," in Mário Baptista Coelho (ed.), *Portugal: O Sistema Político e Constitucional, 1974-1987* (Lisbon: Instituto de Ciências Sociais, 1989); and *A Lei de Defesa Nacional e das Forças Armadas (Textos, discursos e trabalhos preparatórios)* (Coimbra: Coimbra Editora, 1983).

9. No recent publication symbolizes more effectively the coming of age of the social sciences in Portugal than the publication of *Portugal: O Sistema Político e Constitucional 1974-1987*, ed. Mário Baptista Coelho (Lisbon: Instituto de Ciências Sociais, 1989 (1044 pp.).

10. For a fascinating account of the guerrilla actions of civilians in the north of Portugal after the Napoleonic invasions of the Iberian peninsula, see Carlos de Azeredo, *As populações a norte do Douro e os franceses em 1808 e 1809* (Porto: Museu Militar do Porto, 1984).

5

The Aftermath of
Civil-Military Accord:
Institutionalizing a Democratic Regime

If civil-military relations are placed in the broader setting of the accomodations achieved in Portugal since 1976, it should be clear that democratic rule has come to Portugal neither through a settlement confined to civilian elites nor a convergence of interests within the country's political class. There is a fundamental reason why this is the case and it speaks to conditions present in civil society elsewhere in the European periphery. The long history of the domination of society by elite groups, coupled with the exclusion of the masses, produced a situation whereby once radical political change became an option and mass political mobilization had occurred, only a minority of the citizenry had any interest in returning to the politics of exclusion that had characterized all prior regimes, be they authoritarian or democratic.[1]

The revolution which swept across Portugal in 1974 destroyed the old order. It left a badly divided country and considerable institutional disarray that precluded any form of elite agreement as a sufficient base on which to build a new regime. Still, no matter how poorly government functioned in the aftermath and how severe the economic dislocations experienced, few wished to return to the old regime in which in exchange for order and security one had to sacrifice personal freedom and the opportunity to improve one's social condition.

What has been taking place in Portugal since 1976 is a sequence of partial settlements. Seen separately, these settlements really have been little more than transitory agreements over procedures designed to limit conflict and to establish a modus vivendi among contending political forces. They extend from the late 1970s, across the 1980s, to the 1990s. Often interpreted as a demonstration of instability and indicative of the failure of democratic procedures to take root in Iberia, this institutional fluidity and constant reshuffling of political leaders, however, had the cumulative effect of producing a political environment in which procedural democracy came to provide the accepted medium through which radically different political agendas for state and society could be debated and accomodations reached without bloodshed. This setting, in turn, created an appropriate environment within which political leaders could tackle, one by one, policy issues of great import.[2]

Only now, as Portugal entered the 1990s, with this process largely complete, has it become apparent how successful this country's postrevolutionary leadership—military as well as civilian—has been in building consensus over the desirability of democratic procedures in the midst of great social and economic disparities. If the military equation is excluded and confined to the period 1974-82, the sequence of these patterns is lost. Seen together and merged with military affairs, they offer an explanation for what has been achieved.

Portuguese experience is instructive in comparing transitions in Europe and Latin America in yet another sense. For those who would argue that an essential prior condition in the consolidation of democracy is a certain level of socioeconomic development, it is important to point out that this is a society, long isolated on the European periphery, which has always had to face considerable resource constraint and which has experienced marked divisions along class lines between elites and masses. There the historic response to underdevelopment has been elite accommodation with the dominant powers and extensive emigration for those outside the prevailing social order.[3]

In order to defuse what had become an explosive situation as a consequence of revolution, after 1976 Portuguese leaders sought to work out new institutional arrangement quietly, on their own, while continuing to attract sufficient international support to finance the transformations needed. In the context of the new Europe that is emerging in the aftermath of the collapse of Marxist-Leninist regimes to the east and a Latin America in transition to the west, where really very few countries have been able to sideline the military effectively and resource constraints are equally great, this experience is instructive for those committed to realizing democratic ideals in the midst of difficult economic and social conditions. In the Portuguese case, institutionalizing democratic procedures has proven to be the most effective way to overcome past differences and to avoid repeating a history of factionalism, military insubordination, economic instability, social conflict, and recourse to authoritarianism.[4]

Protracted Accords and Sequential Accommodations

Portugal's transition from the fluidity of the revolutionary situation surrounding the breakdown of institutionalized authoritarian rule in 1974, to the stability of a fully consolidated democracy in 1990, took fifteen years. The landmarks in this protracted transition are the two pacts between the armed forces and the parties of April 11, 1975, and February 26, 1976; the constitution of April 2, 1976; and the constitutional revisions of November and December 1982 and of May and June 1989.[5] Each of these agreements focused on the resolution of a significant issue dividing a particular set of political forces, excluded other significant actors, and set up a transitory set of arrangements subject to redefinition once the designation of who the key players were changed. It was not until the end of 1989 that all major actors in post-authoritarian Portugal had accepted procedural democracy as the framework most appropriate for regulating and structuring Portuguese politics for the foreseeable future.

The first pact (I Pacto MFA-Partidos), signed on April 11, 1975, occurred at the high point of the revolution, in the context of a strong reaction against the failed countercoup of March 11 and a government determined to enact more radical policies. Yet even then, at the apex of radical military power linked closely with like-minded civilian forces, it was clear that a plurality of political parties, representing various constellations of leaders and mass followings, had become an integral part of the new political scene. At no point was it possible for military and civilian radicals to consolidate power solely in their hands—hence, the need for political accord. This first agreement, thus, established a bifurcated governmental system in which civilian and military affairs were to remain separate. In the former representation was given to a plurality of parties in a national assembly—the Assembly of the Republic—while in the latter representation was given to the nation's armed forces through its own armed forces assembly—the Assembly of the Armed Forces' Movement. Far from a satisfactory solution to the institutional vacuum that had developed with the collapse of the Estado Novo, this represented a tentative first step in redefining civil-military relations in post-1974 Portugal. It involved the major players at the time: the military officers who had led the coup—the Armed Forces Movement (Movimento das Forças Armadas, MFA)—and the political parties that had come to the fore in the aftermath of the coup of April 25, 1974. The issue at stake at this point was how to restructure civil-military relations, for without an accord between military and civilian leaders no progress could be made in filling the institutional vacuum that had developed. Considerable chaos, conflict, and uncertainty had emerged as a consequence of ill-defined relationships among the Junta of National Salvation which intended to act as a a self-appointed new government, a competing civilian government with prime minister and cabinet, and the armed forces, especially those who had led the coup under the designation known as the Armed Forces Movement. Whereas military officers in the Junta and the MFA had sought to redefine politics in their own terms (albeit without achieving any consensus among themselves), by 1975 with the Junta and the Government redefined as the same collective executive organ it was also clear that the political parties were and would remain key players. No less diverse in an ideological spectrum running from left to right, their power lay in their ability to mobilize mass support. To avoid armed conflict it became obvious that these power contenders would have to negotiate an agreement. Hence, the first pact established a framework within which politics could be conducted for the time being without bloodshed.

The second pact (the II Pacto of February 16, 1976) reflected the outcomes of November 25. In this agreement a MFA now purged of its radical officers and dominated by those sympathetic to social democracy recognized a single national assembly with elected political party representatives, committed the signatories to the election of a president by universal and direct suffrage, and confined military influence to a Council of the Revolution (CR) in which counsellors elected by the armed forces were given constitutional oversight authority. Although it was like the first agreement in its bringing together key military and civilian actors and getting them to realize that neither had the power to dispense with the other, its core constituency was quite different. While the first pact included committed revolutionaries as key players—the left-wing of the MFA, the Portuguese Communist Party (PCP), and other radical political groups—the second pact marginalized military and civilian radicals and brought to the foreground social democratic forces within the military and the civilian parties. The failure of the revolutionary left to bring about mass insurrection on November 25, 1975, and the successful military countercoup led by General António Ramalho Eanes had changed the course of the revolution decisively. This second pact reflected that realignment and opened the way to the negotiation of a new constitutional document that would establish a working relationship among the political forces then dominant in Portugal.

From 1976 until 1982 considerable uncertainty surrounded Portugal's democratic politics. Seen from the vantage point of these years, Portugal's new regime was unstable and tentative. In essence, the country was governed by a dual executive—a president with a national constituency who was also head of the nation's armed forces and a prime minister, with a cabinet, reflecting majority political party alignments in parliament. Gradually emphasis shifted toward civilian primacy. The key players influencing this shift were General Eanes (as head of the armed forces), Mário Soares (as leader of the Socialist Party, PS), Francisco Sá Carneiro (of the Social Democratic Party, the PSD), and Diogo Freitas do Amaral (of the conservative Social Democratic Center, CDS), plus members of the political entourages surrounding these personalities. Accommodation took place first through agreement among these leaders that substantive legislation and control of the budget would be the exclusive domain of the Government (i.e., the prime minister and cabinet). Accountable to the Assembly of the Republic, such Governments would continue in office only so long as they could martial majority support from within that parliamentary body. Over time these men also reached a second informal understanding that all cabinet members, including the Defense Minister, would be civilians.[6]

If the aforementioned outcomes are kept in mind, then the significance of the 1982 constitutional revisions should not be minimized. For this third agreement represented a carefully crafted accord among key civilian and military players whereby civilian primacy was given constitutional sanctioning. After this point, pursuant to full consultation with the armed forces headed up by Freitas do Amaral as defense minister and with their compliance assured by General Eanes, the nation's armed forces were placed under civilian authority. Through these negotiations and extensive public debate, the practice of separately constituted civilian and military affairs inaugurated in the first military-civilian pact in 1975 came to an end. The vehicles for accomplishing all this were two major changes in the Constitution: 1) the abolition of the Council of the Revolution, coupled with the replacement of its judicial review functions by a Constitutional Tribunal, and 2) the promulgation of a National Defense Law that became part of the nation's constitutional charter. Indicative of the extent to which the military would honor its commitment to Portugal's civilian leadership by subjecting itself to civilian control was President Eanes' stance on the final version of the law passed by the Assembly of the Republic. While in disagreement with clauses limiting the power of the president to select the head of the General Staff and shifting military oversight authority to the Government (the prime minister and cabinet), he accepted as legitimate the Assembly's vote on this matter. When the Assembly overrode his veto of the law, he did not reverse his position. Rather, both he and the heads of the armed services let it be known that, while in disagreement with the language of the final law, they recognized it as legitimate and binding on the nation's armed forces.

Implementation of this new accord, however, was not easily accomplished. It was not until Soares as prime minister came to blows with Eanes in July 1983 over the right of the Government to approve or disapprove an action by the Army head in designating a military commander for troops in the north, that the question of military subordination to civilan preferences was finally resolved. Faced with an institutional crisis and a personal stand off between president and prime minister, the principals (Eanes and Soares) ultimately resolved their differences by agreeing that members of the General Staff of the Armed Forces (the Estado Maior Geral das Forças Armadas, EMGFA) would serve only when they held the confidence of both the Government and the President. In the case of future appointments or dismissals below armed forces heads, it was also agreed that the principle of reciprocity would be respected by president and prime minister. No such appointments would occur in the future without the concurrence of both.

The final agreement contributing to the consolidation of Portugal's new democracy has been economic in nature. But this issue could only be dealt with successfully once civil-military relations had been redefined and consensual unity over the procedures to be followed in resolving conflict had been worked out. This accord has involved primarily the leadership of the Socialist and Social Democratic Parties in the Assembly of the Republic, and the key player in this event has been Aníbal Cavaco Silva. Despite his 1987 electoral victory and the formation of Portugal's first majority government under PSD leadership, it was not possible for the Social Democrats to achieve their goal of reversing the nationalizations of 1975 without the cooperation of the PS. Earlier attempts in 1988 by the Cavaco Silva Government to introduce labor reform legislation had generated the largest general strike in the nation's history on March 28 and it was clear that nothing could be achieved in this domain without the cooperation of the Socialists.

Negotiations between the parliamentary blocs of the two parties extended over the last half of 1988 and into the first half of 1989. Eventually what emerged was a coalition involving the support of all the major parties, except the PCP.[7] It affirmed the country's commitment to a mixed market economy and permitted the Government to move ahead with its project of privatizing the nation's banks and insurance companies. Through constitutional revisions executed in May 1989, the irreversibility of the nationalizations carried out at the high point of the revolution in 1975 was canceled by removing article 83, the clause originally written into the constitution to lock in these changes. Subsequently, after much greater debate and a slimmer majority supported only by deputies affiliated with center and center-right political alignments, the Government was successful the next month in getting the Assembly to ratify removal of the commitment to socialism, in article 2, as a goal of the Portuguese state.

Through accomplishing these changes, the Government was able to send a clear signal to the private sector. By ending the constraints placed on the private sector in the original document and opening up the nation's banks and insurance companies to domestic private ownership, private sector interests were assured a major voice in the new order. The symbolic effect of these economic changes has been enormous since at the heart of the grievances expressed in 1974, 1975, and 1976 was the issue of the distribution of economic resources, with advocates of socialism arguing for a strongly state-regulated economy and those of liberal democracy fighting for the creation of competitive market conditions that would make Portugal's economic modernization possible and protect private property.

Conclusion

The centrality of civil-military relations in the transitions in Brazil and the Southern Cone and the extensiveness of the economic cleavages present in the Eastern European regimes make these events and outcomes in Portugal since 1974 especially relevant. Thus, while Portuguese experience remains apart from all the other transitions in Southern Europe and Latin America during the 1970s and 1980s, the issues raised there, the absence of a single overarching settlement, and the way in which cleavages accumulated across the twentieth century have been undone on an issue by issue basis has far greater relevance than Portugal's small size and peripheral location on the European continent would suggest.[8] But, while these accomplishments are great and attention should be directed to them, it is equally important to understand that they were accomplished at the cost of destroying the coherency of the state apparatus present at the time of the coup, through which the old regime had executed the policies with which it was most concerned.

At this point attention now needs to be shifted to the Portuguese state, with clarification forthcoming as to the extent of state autonomy present in today's Portugal. For, unless there is an increase in the state's capacity to implement effectively new policy initiatives, it is unlikely that Portugal will achieve that breakthrough in economic terms so necessary for raising levels of living for the majority of its citizens and for reducing the disparity in incomes which has left Portugal a divided society with major unresolved social issues.

Notes

1. For a clarification of this point regarding the shift in Portugal from a society of limited participation to mass participation in the mid-1970s, see my article "Is the Portuguese Revolution Dead?," *Luso-Brazilian Review*, 16:2 (Winter 1979).

2. The book that most effectively presents the view questioning the consolidation of democratic institutions in Iberia is Howard Wiarda's *The Transition to Democracy in Spain and Portugal* (Lanham, MD: American Enterprise Institute for Public Policy Research, 1989).

3. This particular pattern in Portugal's political economy has been captured most effectively in Elizabeth Leeds, "Labor Export, Development, and the State: The Political Economy of Portuguese Emigration," unpublished doctoral dissertation (Cambridge, MA: Massachusetts Institute of Technology, 1984).

4. For those not familiar with Portuguese political history and the past that current leadership groups have wished to transcend, it is important to understand that authoritarian rule in their experience has not always been equated with political and economic stability. A major contribution in clarifying these dimensions is Douglas Wheeler's *A Ditadura Militar Portuguesa (1926-1933)* (Mém Martins, Portugal: Publicações Europa-América, 1986). The seven years of military rule, albeit equally authoritarian as Salazar's, which preceded the consolidation of the Estado Novo (the civilian dictatorship dominant from 1934 until 1974) proved to be as unstable and volatile as the civilian regime it replaced (the First Republic, 1910-1926).

5. For an excellent discussion of the democratic transition in Portugal, down to 1986, see: Manuel Braga da Cruz, "A Evolução das Instituições Políticas: Partidos Políticos e Forças Armadas na Transição Democrática Portuguesa (1974-1986)," *Povos e Culturas*, no. 1 (1986), pp. 205-15. In this article Braga da Cruz calls attention to the nature of the agreements reached in the two pacts between the military and the parties, specifies the content of the institutional transition taking place 1976-1982, and discusses the "civilianization" of the regime 1982-1986.

6. The significance of this distinction between the civilianization of political power between 1976 and 1982, with the military serving as guarantors of Portugal's new democracy, and the disengagement of the military from politics accompanied by acceptance of civilian rule after 1982 is most clearly stated by José Medeiros Ferreira in "Um corpo perante o Estado: militares e instituições políticas," in *Portugal: O Sistema Política e Constitucional*, pp. 427-51. A closely related discussion of the intent behind the constitutional revisions of 1982 and the changes incorporated at this point in civil-military relations is to be found in Diogo Freitas do Amaral, "A Constituição e as Forças Armadas," in *Portugal*, pp. 647-61.

7. The actual line-up of the voting consisted of the PSD, PS, and CDS in favor of the removal of Article 83 and the PCP, PRD, the Greens and the Independents supporting its retention.

8. An expansed version of this discussion of partial settlements, extended over the last 15 years, as the most effective means for consolidating a democratic regime in a divided society is to be found in my chapter, "Redefining the Portuguese Transition to Democracy," in John Higley and Richard Gunther (eds.), *Elites and Democratic Consolidation in Latin America and Southern Europe* (New York: Cambridge University Press, 1991).

6

Governance in Post-1974 Portugal: Difficulties in Reconstituting the State After Regime Collapse

The institutional consequences of the Portuguese transition to democracy are far-reaching. Whereas before 1974 the Portuguese state played a central role in controlling and regulating politics and markets, since 1974 it has been superseded and bypassed—first in the rush to open up society and subsequently in the endeavor to create a market economy and to stimulate new economic growth. Over the last decade and a half, as a consequence, myriad new actors have entered the world of government and politics—individually, through new leadership roles in the national assembly, the presidency of the republic, and local governments (all determined by elections); and collectively, through the emergence of mass-based party organizations and associations representing a wide variety of interests in civil society.[1]

Paralleling these political developments is extensive, and generally successful, economic change. The creation of a new business environment has in turn led to the demand for and the establishment of new managerial training programs. Seen from this perspective, there can be no doubt about the fact that Portugal's entrance into the European Community in 1986 has altered economic perspectives and outlooks fundamentally. Articles on Portuguese finance, trade, and commerce in the *Economist* and the *Financial Times* have consistently commented on the new dynamism present in the economy.[2]

As a consequence of these economic changes, the structure of Portuguese society also has evolved significantly. As social forces have been liberated and initiatives developed outside the central government, the old pattern of state-society relationships has disappeared. Instead of a state apparatus impeding individual actions and initiatives, citizens are generally free to pursue their own interests. Furthermore, at the local level, a new relationship between political leaders and citizenship groups has emerged. While many central government ministries have remained aloof from these changes, the invigoration of local authorities (*autarquias locais* on the mainland and regional governments on the Atlantic islands) has permitted parallel governments to develop outside the center, involving local communities directly in improving public services of immediate benefit to them.

While all these developments are positive and have contributed to the consolidation of a democratic regime, the record is a mixed one regarding the state. Certainly important changes have occurred in the state apparatus. Among them are the decentralization of political power, the creation of multiple decision-making centers, and the imposition of constraints on unrestrained executive authority. Replacing an authoritarian system of governance, in which the prime minister and the office supporting his work (the *presidência do conselho*) controlled politics and policy, is a regime of divided authority and shared governmental competencies involving the Presidency of the Republic, the Office of the Prime Minister, and the Assembly of the Republic. Coupled with these new institutional arrangements at the center are legal guarantees of regional and local autonomy and consistent support within the Assembly making this autonomy meaningful through the transfer of public funds to sub-national authorities.

While this diffusion of power has provided multiple channels through which participation and public contestation of issues can take place, neither coherent nor effective action in governmental programs can easily be achieved in this setting. The guarantee of meaningful sub-national representation and governance has opened up a significant new arena for expressing and resolving local and regional issues. Yet, communities have found it difficult to obtain sustained benefits from central governmental programs, especially for those disadvantaged by the changes underway. In addition, there is an absence of intermediary structures between central and local governments. Because district governors were so closely identified with authoritarian controls over local affairs, today these officials have only symbolic powers and there is no effective way at the district level to broker the needs of individual localities with central government ministries whose services are administered on a district or regional basis.

The stasis identified with Caetano's last cabinets (*governos*) meant that severe deficiencies in implementing policy were well entrenched on the eve of the revolution. These administrative and bureaucratic weaknesses have been compounded by the political changes that followed the revolution. While the problem presented by the autonomy of political and administrative institutions is hardly new, not only are the constraints on effective policy implementation far greater today, they also have far greater significance. This is because the economic change that has accompanied economic integration into the European Community will now require much more effective governmental response in policy formulation and in program and project implementation in order to meet the standards in quality control and the open competition that entered into effect as of January 1, 1993, when transitional agreements and protection of the Portuguese market ended.

Even more important is the social question, on hold for over a decade, which ultimately will force the government to take a more active role in ensuring equitable distribution of goods and services in an economy at the margins of more dynamic European growth centers. Compared with its neighbor, Spain, Portugal is still far from the threshold crossed by Spain in the 1980s when it gained recognition as a high-income economy and member of the OECD. In contrast, Portugal remains part of the middle-income countries on the European periphery, along with Greece, the Eastern European states, Turkey, and the North African countries.[3]

Alterations in the State Apparatus

Before calling further attention to the bureaucratic obstacles to economic modernization, one should keep in mind how much the institutional setting of the state has changed since 1974.[4] The state which existed before the military coup of April 25 and two years of revolutionary upheavals (1974-1976) was a very different entity. This point warrants emphasis, for the continuities in nomenclature and legal designations often lead outside observers to comment on the immutability of the Portuguese state and bureaucratic practices stretching back across the years.

Four decades of authoritarian rule and administrative change consonant with the concentration of power in the hands of the prime minister did produce a state with well-institutionalized procedures for centralized decision-making on all important issues of public policy as well as effective mechanisms for excluding consideration of these issues most troubling to the dictatorship. Portuguese government before 1974 was in many respects an administrative state in which coordination and control emanated from a single center: the office and the person of the prime minister. This "New State" (Estado Novo) replaced and superseded the weak state characteristic of the First Republic (1910-1926) and the Military Dictatorship (1926-1933).[5]

A single example will suffice to capture the policy environment characteristic of authoritarian Portugal. While the colonial question was of central importance to all major groups in Portugal, within the system as well as outside, the Governments of Marcello Caetano (Salazar's successor, 1969-1974) were able to exclude any open discussion of this issue until the eve of the revolution. Discussion of colonial issues, however, did occur within the corridors of power where participation was restricted to those who accepted the premise for involvement in policy decisions: the integrity of Portuguese overseas territory. When the Government finally permitted General Spínola to publish his ideas for the creation of a Portuguese commonwealth to replace the colonial system, it was too late. Not only were his ideas no longer feasible, in the context of an irreversible movement toward independence for Portuguese Africa, but also it was only a question of time before a captains' movement was to overthrow the regime itself, sideline the military hierarchy of which he was a part, and liberate the colonies.

If the Portuguese state of this era is examined from the standpoint of the centralized decision-making processes and issues dominating the governmental agenda before 1974, it was for all effective purposes a centralized bureaucratic empire in which considerable effort and resources had been invested in linking two key regions in Africa—Angola and Mozambique—with decision-making centers in Lisbon. Once the regime was overthrown and independence of the overseas territories was guaranteed, huge adjustments had to be made. Not only was an extensive administrative apparatus radiating outward from the Ministry of the Overseas (*Ministério do Ultramar*) dismantled overnight, but also overseas agents of the state, as public functionaries with legal guarantees of government employment, were brought home and absorbed into the home service. While figures vary greatly on the number of Portuguese citizens returning to continental Portugal and the proportion of civil servants absorbed by government, it is probably accurate to say that some seven percent of the 600,000 returning to the mainland were considered public employees and thereby entitled to continued public employment.[6]

Ending State Autonomy and Centralization of Power

These autonomous and repressive state structures did not survive the double impact of the radical phase of the revolution (1974-1976), with its emphasis on purging old regime bureaucrats, and the rise of party government (1976-1986). The Governments in power during 1974 and 1975 moved quickly to dismantle the policy-making core of the old state and to destroy all internal security controls. While the overall unitary structure of the state did survive, new leaders also drew up regional autonomy statutes for the Azores and Madeira islands. On the continent, however, the push toward decentralization focused on revitalizing existing local government institutions (*concelhos municipais, juntas de freguesia*, and local development authorities). Despite much public debate concerning the desirability of regionalization, agreement on how to establish regional governments for the mainland proved elusive.

The change in local government, as a consequence of the revolution, is especially notable. Before the revolution, local authorities were an integral part of executive-centered institutions and answered to a tier of public authorities controlled through the Ministry of Internal Administration. Afterwards, local councils became self-governing, representative bodies giving full expression to popular wishes and demands from within the local communities to whom they were now accountable. As a matter of fact, during the radical phase of the revolution, one of the first acts linked to mass mobilization was the seizure of local units of government in the name of the people by citizens and the establishment of people's councils. Later, as the radical phase of the revolution passed and elections became the vehicle for selecting local authorities, local elections became a lively contest among competing individuals and groups.

The outcome of these events has been a hybrid system of governance, sanctioned by the Constitution of 1976, with two tiers of elected officials as well as two distinct sets of national and local institutions. Complementing these political institutions is a much older administrative system consisting of powerful central ministries housed in Lisbon with minimal representation in outlying areas. In such a setting, local authorities frequently find themselves without the capacity to respond effectively to the demands for improved public services in the areas under their jurisdiction, since so many of these activities fall within the domain of ministerial action. At the outset, in 1975, it seemed that innovation in the form of mobile technical assistance teams—the Gabinetes de Apoio Técnico (GAT)—would serve to bridge this gap. But, as this new system of governance became institutionalized and coordination responsibilities for the Gabinetes were vested in regional planning commissions under the control of the central administration, local authorities found the GATs far less likely to respond directly to local needs.[7]

Accompanying the dispersal of authority at the local level has been a pulverization of the state apparatus in the center. From 1974 through 1976, the reaction against centralized bureaucratic controls moved in two directions: continual institutional changes and turnovers in governmental personnel. Public organizations created to maintain the New State were dismantled quickly.

The first of these—the Presidency of the Council of Ministers—was a supraministry created by Salazar, vested with all the control and coordination functions deemed important by the premier. While official forms were maintained, the Presidency of the Council re-emerged as a small staff unit supporting the prime minister. Without any of the powers of coordination and control characteristic of the much larger and more powerful unit serving Salazar and Caetano, it is today a very different public organization.

The second institution to be dismantled, the Ministry of Corporations, was essentially an organ for controlling social policy, which organized and regulated social groups (other than business interests) and provided social programs for them, corporately. The only surviving units of this organization after 1975 were the directorates responsible for labor relations and social security. But, their roles have changed so radically that for all effective purposes they have become very different operations in the new Labor Ministry, as agencies at the service of labor rather than as bureaucratic devices for controlling labor.

The third institution to be dismantled was internal security. Housed in an autonomous office, called the Direcção Geral de Segurança (DGS)—the Directorate General for Security, it was known originally as PIDE (the Policia Internacional de Defesa do Estado) during the Salazar era. Under Caetano it received a new name but little else changed; it continued to answer directly to the prime minister and retained an effective surveillance apparatus of its own reaching throughout the mainland and the overseas territories. More than any other institution it symbolized the repression characteristic of the old regime. Not surprisingly, its abolition was definitive.

The last of these organizations slated for replacement, the Overseas Ministry, consisted of directorates-general matching each of the domestic ministries. These bureaus oversaw corresponding sets of activities overseas. These were administered through regional governments, operating at the provincial level. Usually headed by military officers, civilian authorities were housed within these units of governance. While some of these civilian bureaucrats were granted general oversight authority, others served as representatives of central directorates, under provisions of dual authority and supervision. With the independence of the overseas territories, this central ministry disappeared, although its provincial units survived in many instances through cooperants (cooperantes) or Africans who sought to fill the power vacuum left by the departure of the colonial bureaucracy.

Collective action, by individuals within the civil service, accompanied external popular pressures to liquidate the control mechanisms identified with these organizations, especially those of the DGS and the local police. Office workers joined hands with external political groups to remove directors and directors-general, through a process known as saneamento (cleansing). Whereas Salazar had used the same procedures in the late 1920s and the early 1930s to "cleanse" the public service of senior bureaucrats identified with republican and liberal perspectives, the gonçalvistas—those military officers and civilians identified with the premiership of Captain (later General) António Vasco dos Santos Gonçalves—employed the same technique to remove those identified with the authoritarian, corporatist, and repressive practices of the Estado Novo. In their place, each new political group taking control of the state apparatus made partisan political appointments of its own, to ensure the execution of its programs according to party dictates. Replacing the gonçalvistas dominant in 1974-76 were Socialist party militants in the late 1970s. In turn, PSD activists layered in their supporters throughout the 1980s.

The Consequences of Partisanship in a Semi-Presidential System

The impact of these actions from above and popular initiatives from below was sufficient to paralyze the state as an effective instrument through which to execute and implement policy. This was especially the case during 1974-1976—when mass mobilization and the occupation of places of work, vacant housing, and land introduced an element of uncertainty over which no one in government really had effective control.[8] During these years, political movements outside government, in alliance with sympathetic government employees, organized worker commissions which took over specific offices and departments.

Under these pressures, a twofold process ensued. At the senior management level tenured civil servants (directors and the directors-general) left public employment, while at the middle and lower levels new employees moved into public positions with each major cabinet change. Simultaneously, various secretaries of state (*secretários de estado*) blanketed returning overseas civil servants into the central government's home civil service, while at the local level the new political parties taking power brought into office political partisans whom they could count on in mounting new services of interest to their new-found clienteles. Then, as the extremes of the revolution waned, older civil servants—purged earlier from office—returned to reclaim positions guaranteed to them under public law as tenured state employees. Political clientelism (the blanketing into public jobs of one's own political following) coupled with the recognition of the employment rights of public employees with the status of *funcionários* led to a rapid expansion in the number of the people working for the state. To these numbers must also be added those who worked in private sector organizations nationalized by the government or transferred to the public domain as a consequence of bankruptcy or the exit of these firms' previous owners between 1974 and 1976. Hence, whereas the central administration reported 155,200 in 1968 (the last public employee census before the revolution), by 1979 the total had increased to 313,800 and by 1983, to 442,000. At the local and regional level, the increase was from 41,542 in 1968 to 58,266 in 1979 and to 72,562 in 1983.[9]

This increase in public sector employment, when coupled with expansion in the number of state-owned enterprises and the absence of central controls, destroyed the coherency of the old administrative system without providing a substitute. In this context public administration drifted across 1975 and 1976 into 1977 and 1978. Although President Eanes attempted to bring about administrative reform during the era of the technocratic cabinets (summer 1978 through fall 1979), none of the party-based Governments since has given anything other than lip service to the prospects of administrative reform. The more important issues concerned the constitution of new political institutions and questions of accountability and control between the Presidency of the Republic and the Assembly of the Republic, in which parliamentary Governments headed by a succession of prime ministers reflected continually shifting party alignments among the deputies.

While this divergence between national political and administrative institutions is serious, the hiatus between political and administrative structures is greatest at the local level. There, since 1975, specific programs and activities have had to be carried out within a spatial context that superimposes numerous public officials. These consist of civil governors, whose powers are now emasculated but retain responsibilities for political regions known as *distritos*, regional representatives of the central government in planning units staffed by regional subordinates in key population centers, field officials representing self-contained central ministries, and local authorities occupying public positions in individually constituted local assemblies and administrative institutions. The consequence has been a disjointed set of intergovernmental relations, characterized by three patterns.

First, field agencies of the central government remain constrained by the concentration of decision-making authority in Lisbon and, to a lesser extent, in such regional centers as Porto and Coimbra. Not only is funding for these agencies at the sub-national level as limited today as in the past, but field representatives have even less capacity today to influence local affairs, because of autonomous local governments. Under the Estado Novo, central government agencies were charged with significant regulatory functions and few activities could be initiated at the local level without obtaining approval from government officials outside the community.

These changes in local governance since 1974 thus have produced mixed results. On the one hand, local autonomy and local self-government have given new vitality to community life. Because of their accountability to local electorates, local authorities are much more likely to seek to maximize those activities which give credit to their claims to be exercising public office in accord with responsiveness to public demands. But, the primary public goods needed to enact these services fall in the area of fiscal and technical resources external to the community. Some of these are available through field agency officials, representing the central ministries. Others come from offices and programs identified with the European Community. But, whatever the source, they remain external resources whose allocations are driven by priorities and interests external to the communities receiving them.

Second, municipal councils usually lack adequate professional staffs of their own to provide either new or expanded public services. While strong on representation, local councils and mayors have little or no influence over the local economy and their capacity to extract new monetary resources is as limited today as in the past. Economic change thus remains conditioned by external resources provided by the central government and, more and more, according to terms set by the European Community in exchange for financing local projects. The primary source for operating funds for local authorities, however, is the Assembly of the Republic and the provisions it makes for transfers to local governments in the annual budget.

Third, public officials and organizations serving as intermediaries between center and periphery are equally short of funds, technical staff, and influence. They have the capacity neither to respond to local needs nor leverage much policy coherency at the local level when instances arise of competing and overlapping activities. Because civil governors before the revolution were essentially representatives of the central government with strong powers to oversee and control local affairs, there has been little interest since in vesting them with new authority. Their powers today are largely symbolic, as representatives of the Government in office, and the only real influence they have over local affairs is a function of their own individual personalities and whether or not they can convince others that they have a useful brokerage role to play.

Thus, while the new political system is responsive to voter preferences and gives representation to a diversity of interests, the state apparatus is weak in its capacity to implement programs and to execute responsibilities assigned to it by the Government in power. Indicative of this situation are citizen perceptions of the performance of governmental institutions, as reflected in a 1985 survey conducted by the Marketing and Public Opinion Division of NORMA (a Lisbon firm). This survey was designed to obtain a representative sample of citizen attitudes regarding the quality of public services and their efficacy. Generally speaking, many of these results confirmed what popular news sources had been reporting in the 1980s: an overall deterioration in public services provided by central government ministries. But a more careful perusal of these data also shows some interesting variations in service delivery, when the state apparatus is disaggregated into individual public organizations according to region and type of public service provided. Generally speaking, one can note a perception that services have improved where public organizations have developed an awareness of the importance of the interests of the groups they are serving.[10]

In this particular survey, 995 individuals were interviewed randomly throughout Portugal. This information is recorded in Table 6.1. Eight questions, regarding different types of public service, were directed at the public. These questions ranged from whether or not the individual felt that the service in question had improved, worsened, or remained the same. These data are recorded in Table 6.2.

Those public services which are provided by central government ministries through field offices, in Table 6.2, are (1) public health services, (2) social security, and (3) tax collection. These are all instances where service delivery responds essentially to hierarchical norms. While the official is certainly aware of and in direct contact with the public, the work environment is structured more by the public organization of which he or she is an employee than by responsiveness to external groups receiving these services. In these three cases the perception revealed by the survey is that the services provided have worsened since 1974, especially outside the center. In some cases the contrast in the perception of the quality of service performed before and after the revolution is dramatic. In others, the differences are less marked. In still others—especially in Lisbon (LIS.) and Porto (PTO.)—services have either remained much the same or improved.

Whereas the first three vertical entries in Table 6.2 are central government directed and controlled, the remaining five are all performed by public organizations outside the central administration. These are either public enterprises (e.g., TLP—Telefones de Lisboa e Porto—and CTT—Correios e Telecomunicações de Portugal) or services operated by local governments (which are exercised directly by a municipal authority, a separately constituted local public organization, or a cooperative venture supported by a group of local governments). What is present here are two interrelated phenomena. Local government councils generally perceive successful performance of these services to be indicators of their responsiveness to local citizen demands. Similarly public-service oriented state-owned enterprises are apparently more sensitive to citizen demands and the representation of governmental authorities for expanded services than are central government operated services. Hence, here service delivery has improved outside the major cities of Lisbon and Porto. In large part, this has come about as a consequence of more extensive field networks that have brought these enterprises into closer contact with consumers (as, for example, in the expanded services provided by TLP and CTT in response to citizen demands and defense of these requests by local authorities).[11] Again, in these cases as above, patterns vary considerably from one region to another. The most notable exception is in the perception that public transportation and telephone services had worsened in Lisbon and Porto since the revolution.

All in all, what these data support are the interpretation that where meaningful local autonomy exists it has had the effect of expanding basic public services to localities outside the center, where such services were previously deficient or absent and where local authorities are now in a position to press for such services. In these instances public services have improved. But older central ministries and previously existing autonomous public entities constituted before 1974 remain as bureaucratized, as centralized, and as unresponsive to citizen demands as ever.

The Relevancy of the State in Regime Consolidation

Consideration of the interrelationships between political and administrative institutions, first under authoritarianism and later under more open, democratic arrangements, suggests the presence of an important dynamic in analyzing the nature of domestic change and the way in which governments function. Not only does such analysis serve as a corrective to some of the facile generalizations about the performance of authoritarian and democratic regimes, but it also calls attention to the utility of examining the wider institutional setting of the state and how the autonomy of its activities varies according to the content and structure of political regimes. This is a dimension of politics integrating the bureaucratic component with political institutions and civil society warranting particular attention in newly constituted democratic regimes, especially during their consolidation.

In the Portuguese case, neither military nor civilian bureaucracy has been restructured in such a way as to permit them to respond to the new demands on Portuguese government since 1976. While civil-military questions dominated much of the policy agenda from 1976 to 1981 and competition between president and prime minister in defining how a semi-presidential parliamentary system was to operate permeated all policy issues from 1982 to 1987, since 1987 (when the PSD obtained an absolute majority in the Assembly of the Republic) restructuring of the domestic economy has been the Government's central concern.

The consequence of these outcomes—in which civilian oversight authority, the supremacy of party government, and the primacy of economic restructuring have dominated the policy agenda in succeeding order—has been disjointed intergovernmental relations. Certainly one cannot equate centralization of power and decision-making authority with authoritarian governance, on the one hand, and decentralization of power and authority with more democratic regimes, on the other. But, what is equally clear in the Portuguese case is that a significant part of the transition from one regime to the other has entailed increasing the degree of autonomy permitted in the periphery and expanding government services in response to pressures from below.

These developments, however, have had direct impact on the autonomy of the state and the weight of civilian and military bureaucratic institutions. While the question of civil-military relations and its impact on the state was dealt with first, because this was the initial focus of the debate over regime change after 1974, it is equally important to bring in the civilian bureaucratic component to understand the dynamics of the movement from transition to consolidation in Portugal. Bypassed in large part by the changes that have swept across Portugal, many central ministries and their field offices have found their capacity to perform services to be constrained by the external political and economic environment. Nevertheless, these patterns are not always clear and vary tremendously according to the office and program with which one is concerned.

If one takes a comparative, long-term view, what available data and intepretations suggest are that the country has returned to a situation at the end of the twentieth century analogous to the situation it encountered at the beginning of the century, when its Governments were faced with severe limitations on their capacity to act because of a weak state that constrained their ability to carry out effective economic and social policy. This pattern remained largely the same, in the movement from constitutional monarchy to republic and from a limited democracy to military dictatorship, until António Salazar emerged as a powerful independent political actor. The consolidation of his power and his movement from Finance Minister to Prime Minister was tied in with the building of a bureaucratic-authoritarian state independent of political groups and pressures outside the state. But these patterns of politics and administration, while they projected an image of permanence up until the eve of the revolution, proved to be as fluid and as permeable as ever, once the monopoly of power held in the hands of authoritarian prime ministers and their supporters was broken.

The outcome of the 15 years that extend from 1974 to 1989 has been the creation of a political regime strong on representation but weak in its capacity to implement economic and social policy. Seen from this vantage point, the Portuguese state has become, once again, a weak state. Subject now to shifting partisan pressures, it has become responsive to the various clienteles accompanying political personalities as they move from one public office to another.

At the same time, there is one major difference in the present policy environment: Portugal's membership in the European Community (EC) since 1986. Whereas the impact of the Portuguese revolution and the Constitution of 1976 were essentially structural (in that they produced a truncated state still characterized by centralism and hierarchy within individual ministerial organizations but without new mechanisms for coordination and control), the impact of the European Commission (the permanent executive of the European Community) has been more substantive, through the interjection of new economic resources. This has occurred through two mechanisms: economic assistance provided to Portugal as a lesser developed European region and the various regulations and accords commensurate with participation in European markets. Both have required major adjustments in the state apparatus and are certain to increase after 1992, in setting up offices administering funds provided for numerous new programs and projects—be they public works, commercial undertakings, or agricultural initiatives—as well as in restructuring public institutions and procedures related to financial transactions, trade, and investments.

From 1986 onward one has been able to sense a quickening in the rate of economic change all over Portugal, from new credits made available to local governments to improve urban infrastructure, to programs designed to augment agricultural productivity, to improvements in the national highway system. All these activities have, in one way or another, forced change upon different organizations within the state, be it through adjusting central ministerial operations to disburse development funds according to EC guidelines, or creating new offices parallel to older ones to ensure more rapid implementation of programs and projects with European financing, or complying with regulations and policies linked to financial transactions and market reforms. Seen from this perspective, the new reality confronted has entailed making all sorts of changes within the state, albeit on a piecemeal basis, despite appearances to the contrary. As time has passed, the divergence between these new realities and the formalism characteristic of established procedures and continued use of the same, old legal norms regulating civil servant behavior has increased exponentially.[12]

While the previous chapter argued that Portugal's democratic breakthrough created conditions whereby a consolidated democratic regime had emerged by 1989 through negotiated settlement with military actors, this chapter through its concern with policy and management issues in the civilian bureaucracy raises some troubling questions. As long as the present conjunctural situation continues, in which there are ample economic and political supports coming from within the European

Community, these conditions are not likely to place undue pressures on the current leadership. Incremental change can continue to take place through the impact dictated by external resources and conditions negotiated by the Government. But, to the extent that social issues come to the fore and external resources are shifted eastward, the problems of the great inequities present in Portuguese society and the underdevelopment of much of the country, when compared with the affluent consumer societies present in core areas of the Community, will present the Government with difficult choices. When that moment arrives, the capacity of the state to design and implement social and economic policy will become of critical importance. In such a policy environment Portugal will find itself poorly prepared to defend its own national interests, for without a state apparatus capable of interceding effectively between external and internal markets the price to be paid is one of increasing dependency on the decisions of external actors. It is these conditions, coupled with the priority given to economic restructuring at the expense of social policy, that has led Boaventura de Sousa Santos—a prominent Portuguese social scientist—to conclude that the current political class will sooner or later have to face a crisis of regime.[13]

The Future of the State in Portugal

My own conclusion is that as European integration moves ahead and Portugal enters into more intensive economic and political relations with other Community members, it is likely that few of these patterns in the way in which the Portuguese state has evolved will change, unless those controlling current resources decide to take the initiative. Until that time comes, the primary stimulus for change will almost certainly continue to be external to the state, in the context of the externalities discussed above.

At the same time, the pace of change is just as likely to increase, because of the pressures on the Portuguese state to adapt itself more quickly to the norms and policies regulating economic behavior within the Community. Consequently, whereas political support within parliament for administrative reform has been and remains weak, Portugal's presidency of the Community during 1992 coupled with the new mandate given to the PSD Government as a consequence of the last round of parliamentary elections have created the most propitious environment ever for undertaking extensive governmental reorganization.

It is here that questions of political choice enter in, for whether or not change is induced in this area will depend on the present leaders. In light of Portugal's past administrative history, there is nothing inevitable indicating that such action will be taken—especially now that questions of the military reintervening in politics have been laid to rest. This is because policy reform initiatives as well as structural adjustments within state institutions require conscious choice and determination to engage in actions involving costs as well as benefits. Yet, even at a minimum, it is likely that the Secretariat for Administrative Reform and the Instituto Nacional de Administração—the primary organizations charged with action for change in public bureaucracy—will have enhanced opportunities to revamp state institutions and to upgrade performance expectations of civil servants through new training and recruitment initiatives in the years ahead.

Up until this point, basic reform of the state apparatus has been avoided. The changes that have occurred have been a function largely of external conditions and, accordingly, piecemeal in nature. Yet, if Portugal is placed within the context of other contemporary states, one can also argue that major reorganization is now essential if the role of the state as mediator and entrepreneur, in cooperation with the private sector, is to be made compatible with the requirements of political democracy and a market economy. The issue at stake thus becomes not so much one of what is desirable but how to elaborate an appropriate political strategy that will make a reduction in force acceptable. While the figures vary considerably, all accounts of the numbers of employees on the state payroll reflect growth in the size of the public service since 1974, especially if one includes in these figures not just central government personnel but also public employees within local government. Elsewhere, as privatization pressures have increased and more and more public services are having to respond to market criteria, state shrinking issues have emerged. At the same time, cross-national experience has also shown that in creating the economic conditions for greater competitiveness internationally there are important new regulatory and mediatory roles for the state which require a more technically competent and professional civil service, albeit with much smaller office staffs.

What is most significant about Portugal in this regard is that, while major changes have been made over the last decade in private sector management education, corresponding changes in the preparation of men and women for public service careers are difficult to identify, especially in areas linked to public management and policy reform initiatives. Even though resources are tight for education in general, since economic modernization has placed all sorts of demands on restructuring public and private institutions, it is difficult to conceive of changing the state apparatus without giving greater attention to the preparation of a new generation of professionals for public sector work with greater skills in and knowledge of public policy and public management.

Whichever direction Portugal moves in the years ahead in public management education, it is certain that major restructuring of the state, reduction in the size of the public sector, and greater professionalization of its public employees will continue to constitute issues of concern. Such is the pattern that has already become necessary elsewhere in the readjustments all governments are having to make as we are all moving into a new world characterized by the globalization of markets and the internationalization of policy agendas that previously were the exclusive domain of sovereign states.

TABLE 6.1 Distribution of Population Interviewed

	Sample Size	Total Population (in thousands)
Region		
Greater Lisbon	232	1,584
Greater Porto	178	746
The Atlantic Coast (Litoral)	212	2,438
The Interior of the North	178	1,133
The Interior of the South	195	978
Area		
Rural (under 2,000 inhabitants)	250	3,734
Intermediate (2,000-10,000)	198	965
Urban (over 10,000 inhabitants)	547	2,180
Sex		
Male	387	3,301
Female	608	3,578
Age		
18-34 years	296	2,120
35-54 years	360	2,611
55+ years	339	2,148

Source: Divisão de Marketing e Opinião Pública, NORMA (Lisbon: unpublished survey results, May 1985).

TABLE 6.2 Citizen Attitudes on Public Services since 1974

	Total	Gtr. Lis.	Gtr. Pto.	Coast	Int. Nor.	Int. Sou.	Rural	Intr med.	Urban	Porto	Lisbon
Question: Compared with before April 25th, do you consider that:											
1. Public health services:											
Improved:	30.0	34.4	31.9	21.9	31.0	40.1	28.4	29.8	32.7	18.7	29.0
Worsened:	41.0	37.1	38.3	46.2	45.4	31.0	43.4	38.7	37.8	46.5	38.8
Rem. Same:	16.7	20.5	21.6	16.8	7.0	18.2	13.4	23.7	19.4	11.0	18.5
No Opinion:	12.4	8.0	8.2	15.1	16.6	10.8	14.9	7.8	10.1	23.8	13.7
2. Social security:											
Improved:	31.5	45.3	24.9	22.1	31.6	37.3	27.0	25.5	41.8	32.4	31.8
Worsened:	34.5	29.3	49.0	35.7	41.0	21.5	36.5	39.9	28.9	29.8	31.6
Rem. Same:	20.6	17.6	17.7	24.2	8.8	32.1	19.8	27.2	18.8	16.4	22.0
No Opinion:	13.4	7.7	8.3	18.0	18.6	9.1	16.7	7.4	10.5	21.4	14.6
3. Tax collection:											
Improved:	17.0	33.0	12.0	9.0	22.0	9.4	10.8	29.2	22.3	16.3	17.0
Worsened:	48.1	47.9	54.8	47.9	52.3	39.2	50.4	37.9	48.7	40.6	51.8
Rem. Same:	21.1	12.0	22.7	26.7	8.3	35.6	21.5	26.8	17.9	14.3	18.0
No Opinion:	13.7	7.1	10.5	16.5	17.5	15.7	17.2	6.0	11.1	28.9	13.2

4. Water service:

Improved:	41.2	44.6	24.7	41.1	51.6	33.0	44.0	45.2	34.6	22.2	26.5
Worsened:	29.7	31.0	39.0	28.3	25.4	29.1	28.2	27.4	33.3	40.4	38.2
Rem. Same:	18.6	17.9	30.4	16.1	8.7	28.4	14.5	21.4	24.4	20.5	28.3
No Opinion:	10.5	4.5	5.8	14.5	14.4	9.6	13.3	6.0	7.8	16.8	7.0

5. Electrical service:

Improved:	42.3	47.5	24.3	43.0	53.1	33.2	46.3	46.2	33.5	20.2	26.8
Worsened:	31.2	30.9	41.7	28.9	27.4	33.6	30.0	24.0	36.4	46.2	39.7
Rem. Same:	17.9	17.0	29.3	16.4	8.1	26.0	13.5	24.6	22.6	20.0.	28.0
No Opinion:	8.6	4.7	4.7	11.7	11.4	7.1	10.2	5.3	7.5	13.6	5.5

6. Public transportation:

Improved:	37.5	48.8	34.6	27.7	50.3	30.8	36.6	43.7	36.3	33.6	28.1
Worsened:	33.0	31.5	37.7	37.6	24.1	30.9	32.4	27.7	36.6	43.1	45.5
Rem. Same:	18.2	14.6	22.7	19.8	7.8	29.0	17.6	21.2	18.1	10.2	20.0
No Opinion:	11.3	5.1	5.1	14.9	17.8	9.2	13.5	7.4	9.1	13.2	6.5

7. Telephones:

Improved:	36.1	40.9	32.2	30.4	52.0	26.9	37.1	41.4	31.9	23.4	19.6
Worsened:	30.1	35.8	35.8	32.3	26.2	15.8	27.7	27.4	35.5	35.9	45.9
Rem. Same:	20.7	16.1	22.6	22.9	6.3	37.6	20.1	23.4	20.3	17.6	22.9
No Opinion:	13.2	7.3	9.5	14.4	15.5	19.8	15.1	7.9	12.3	23.1	11.6

(continued)

TABLE 6.2 (continued)

	Total	Gtr. Lis.	Gtr. Pto.	Coast	Int. Nor.	Int. Sou.	Rural	Intr med.	Urban	Porto	Lisbon
8. Postal service:											
Improved:	37.4	42.5	31.3	31.1	55.3	28.3	37.6	38.7	36.3	29.1	24.8
Worsened:	22.0	18.5	27.6	24.8	24.9	13.3	24.3	16.9	20.5	16.7	24.4
Rem. Same:	25.6	24.5	27.7	25.7	7.5	47.8	23.7	30.4	27.2	23.8	33.7
No Opinion:	14.8	14.5	13.4	18.4	12.4	10.5	14.4	14.0	16.0	30.4	17.0

Source: Divisão de Marketing e Opinião Pública, NORMA (Lisbon: unpublished survey results, May 1985).

Notes

1. Accompanying this emergence of a new political class of civilians committed to democratic rule, once military officers engaged in politics had been moved to the sidelines, is an extensive body of political studies focused on parties, elections, and the mobilization of mass constituencies. While this literature has become extensive, the materials which give clearest insight into these developments are Thomas C. Bruneau and Alex Macleod, *Politics in Contemporary Portugal* (Boulder, CO: Lynne Rienner Publishers, 1986); Eduardo de Sousa Ferreira and Walter C. Opello, Jr. (eds.), *Conflictos e Mudanças em Portugal, 1974-1984* (Lisboa: Teorema, 1985); "Mudanças Sociais no Portugal de Hoje: Comunicações ao Colóquio Organizado pelo Instituto de Ciências Sociais," *Análise Social*, 21: 87-89 (1985); and "A Formação de Portugal Contemporâneo, 1900-1980, vols. 1-2, *Análise Social*, 18: 72-74 (1982) and 19: 77-79 (1983).

2. While there is an ample professional literature analyzing these alterations, in my estimation the best single source summarizing them is Diana Smith, *Portugal and the Challenge of 1992*, Camões Center Special Report No. 1 (New York: Camões Center, Research Institute on International Change, Columbia University, 1990).

3. See the *World Development Report 1991: The Challenge of Development* (New York: Oxford University Press, 1991), especially the map on pp. 200-1 and Table 1 "Basic Indicators," on pp. 204-5.

4. The issue at stake here concerns state autonomy, which in a comparative setting must be seen as variable, diachronically as well as synchronically. In this regard, it is important to keep in mind that, while I am indebted to the work of Theda Skocpol in rethinking the role of the state in society, I am well aware of its limitations and the need to use the state in comparative context with greater rigor. For a discussion of these issues, see: Bartholomew H. Sparrow, "Review Essay: The State and the Politics of Oil," *Theory and Society*, 20 (1991), pp. 259-81, and "Skocpol and the American State" (unpublished paper) (San Francisco, CA: Annual Meeting of the American Political Science Association, 1990).

5. The weakness of the Portuguese state and the absence of state autonomy in Portugal of the First Republic is most clearly developed in Kathleen C. Schwartzman, *The Social Origins of Democratic Collapse: The First Portuguese Republic in the Global Economy* (Lawrence: University Press of Kansas, 1989). Schwartzman sums up her argument in these

terms: "In this case, we see that the disarticulated economy was the condition under which the state first became more Balkanized and only after the democratic collapse more autonomous" (p. 190). But, it is equally important to understand that the military government established in 1926 inherited a balkanized state apparatus and was equally unable to implement policy. It was only with the accession to power of a civilian economist, António Salazar, that the slow and painful construction of an autonomous state apparatus began first in the creation of an autonomous Finance Ministry and later in its extension to the other organs essential to the consolidation of Salazar's power as prime minister: the Presidência do Conselho (the Prime Minister's Office), the Public Works Ministry, the Ministry of Corporations, and the Overseas Ministry. On the importance of distinguishing between the military dictatorship (1926-1933) and the bureaucratic-authoritarian regime, under civilian authority, known as the New State (1933-1974), see: Douglas Wheeler, *A Ditadura Militar Portuguesa, 1926-1933* (Mém Martins, Portugal: Publicações Europa-América, 1986) and Lawrence S. Graham, *Portugal: The Decline and Collapse of an Authoritarian Order* (Beverly Hills, CA: Sage Professional Papers in Comparative Politics, vol. 1, series no. 01-001, Sage Publications, 1975).

6. Kenneth Maxwell uses the figure of 600,000 in reporting the number of Portuguese settlers who returned to mainland Portugal. See his article, "Regime Overthrow and the Prospects for Democratic Transition in Portugal," in Guillermo O'Donnell, Philippe C. Schmitter, and Laurence Whitehead (eds.), *Transitions from Authoritarian Rule: Southern Europe* (Baltimore: Johns Hopkins University Press, 1986), p. 134. Figures on the numbers of civil servants reincorporated into the home civil service vary between 35,000 and 45,000. For the purposes of this chapter, I would suggest using 40,000 as the approximate figure to match Maxwell's 600,000. See my article "Bureaucratic Politics and the Problem of Reform in the State Apparatus," in Lawrence S. Graham and Douglas L. Wheeler (eds.), *In Search of Modern Portugal: The Revolution and Its Consequences* (Madison: University of Wisconsin Press, 1983), p. 238.

7. For a more complete discussion of center-periphery relations and how they have changed in moving from authoritarian to democratic governance, see my chapter "Center-Periphery Relations," in Kenneth Maxwell and Michael H. Haltzel (eds.), *Portugal: Ancient Country, Young Democracy* (Washington, DC: The Wilson Center Press, 1990).

8. For an excellent discussion of social movements outside the state that developed during the revolution, see: John L. Hammond, *Building Popular Power: Workers' and Neighborhood Movements in the Portuguese Revolution* (New York: Monthly Review Press, 1988).

9. Public employment figures for Portugal are very difficult to pin down and one encounters widescale discrepancies according to the sources used. The most reliable probably are those available from the Secretaria de Estado da Administração Regional and these are the ones reported here, on the basis of the following source: António Barreto, "Estudo central e descentralização: antecedentes e evolução, 1974-84," *Análise Social*, 20: 81-82 (1984), p. 207.

10. See, for example, Thomas C. Bruneau, "Popular Support for Democracy in Post-Revolutionary Portugal: Results from a Survey," in Lawrence S. Graham and Douglas L. Wheeler (eds.), *In Search of Modern Portugal: The Revolution and Its Consequences* (Madison: University of Wisconsin Press, 1983), and *Politics and Nationhood: Post-Revolutionary Portugal* (New York: Praeger Publishers, 1984).

11. See: "Telefones em 84: oferta ultrapassou a procura em 50%," *Expresso* (9 February 1985), p. 13.

12. Much of this discussion and the preceding analysis of civilian bureaucracy draw on material published previously by me in the article "Institutionalizing Democracy: Governance in Post-1974 Portugal," in Ali Farazmand (ed.), *Handbook of Comparative and Development Public Administration* (New York: Marcel Dekker, 1991).

13. Boaventura de Sousa Santos, "A Crise e a Reconstituição do Estado em Portugal (1974-84)," *Revista Crítica de Ciências Sociais*, No. 14 (November 1984), pp. 7-29. For a compilation and updating of his articles published in various Portuguese journals, see his book, *O Estado e a Sociedade em Portugal (1974-1988)* (Porto: Edições Afrontamento, 1990).

7

Transitions in Eastern Europe and Latin America: The Implications of the Portuguese Case

In contrast to the generally successful consolidation of democratic regimes in Southern Europe, the breakdown of authoritarian rule and the transition to more open forms of governance in Latin America and Eastern Europe have led to great uncertainty. There we are far from seeing the creation of a policy environment in which the emergence of party government and commitment to democratic rule are sufficient to guarantee the survival of democratic regimes. Comparative assessment of these transitions suggests instead that economic turbulence, tentative political accords, and qualified military withdrawals from politics will continue to dominate the policy agendas of most of these countries for the foreseeable future. This is especially the case in South America and the Balkans.

Though often neglected in assessments of the Southern European transitions, civilian oversight authority and reform of the state apparatus are issues central to the consolidation and maintenance of democratic regimes. In negotiating a new role for the military, policy makers have generally avoided the question of how to establish and sustain civilian oversight authority over the military. Instead, they have either agreed to exclude discussion of this issue until a later date (the case of Chile) or tacitly concluded that all parties would best be served by the disengagement of the military from civilian politics for the present (the case of Brazil). Reponse to the other issue—reform of the state apparatus and the place of old-regime bureaucrats (civilian as well as military) in the new order—has been even more ambiguous. While new governments have removed those civil servants most closely identified with authoritarian rule and made new appointments to top policy positions, they have been reluctant to engage public sector reform directly. The major exception to this generalization concerns privatization, but even in those instances where extensive privatization is being carried out (for example, Argentina and Poland), the core of the state apparatus has remained untouched.[1]

In this setting Portugal serves as an important bridge case. As I have demonstrated earlier, Portuguese experience, which is seen as the exception to the rule in Southern European transitions, is more instructive and capable of providing insights into the dilemmas confronted in fragmented societies, such as those frequently found today in the Balkans and South America. Like elites in these societies, Portuguese elites have long patterned their modernization endeavors on their perception of what has contributed most to economic and political progress in Western Europe. Yet, their actual experience in economics and politics has left them, more often than not at the margins, within the range of countries often referred to as the European periphery.[2]

Now that the initial euphoria accompanying the collapse of communist regimes in Eastern Europe has passed and it is apparent that difficult political, economic, and social choices must be made, it is timely to return to themes raised originally in the transitions literature. But we need to do so in a much broader and more inclusive context. As new actors seek to establish and consolidate democratic regimes, it has become obvious that greater attention must be given to the linkages between economic and social policy and the political context within which governmental decisions are made. Although scholars of Southern Europe and Southern Cone South America have moved beyond the analysis of transitions to concentrate on regime consolidation and problems arising from disparities in income, deficient social services, and institutional breakdown, none has engaged the issue of how the obstacles to consolidation must be dealt with in order to transcend current stalemates.

While one country's experience can never be fully replicated, many of the dilemmas confronted in Portugal during the 1970s and 1980s have relevancy for other countries now facing difficult economic, social, and political issues in consolidating a democratic regime. As I noted earlier, because there is an ample literature on the activation of pro-democratic forces in civil society and on elections and mass-based parties, I have focused attention on two components hitherto neglected in previous assessments of the Portuguese transition: 1) how the involvement of military leaders in negotiating civilian oversight authority proved absolutely essential in building consensus over democratic rule and 2) the problems engendered by dismantling the old state apparatus without attending to the installation of administrative structures supportive of democratic governance.

In all these transitions, there are three clusters of interests that require redefinition in the aftermath of the collapse of the old regime. First and foremost is the military institution (with its divisions between officers and enlisted men outside the state and those employed within the state apparatus as military bureaucrats). In second place stands the old political class (with its ties to the state apparatus through overlapping appointments and networks involving civilian bureaucrats that provide ready access to economic resources). Third, there is the democratic opposition (divided into an enormous variety of interests and competing perspectives on politics and economics).

Had the Junta of National Salvation been more successful during the early stages of the Portuguese Revolution in reconstituting a new governing coalition and had Spínola been able to isolate younger officers and enlisted men favoring more radical change for a longer period of time, then it might be easier to draw parallels with the Romanian case and to suggest analogous patterns elsewhere in the Balkans. There the National Salvation Front and the Iliescu government have been much more successful in building a coalition centered around the old political class, involving civilian and military bureaucrats who quickly severed their ties with the Ceauşescu regime and have since joined hands with new conservative groups outside the state. As a consequence, one cannot speak of the sudden collapse of the old state apparatus in the Romanian case, as proved to be the case early on with Portugal. But, had Spínola consolidated his coalition more quickly and pre-empted the space later occupied by the MFA, these differences would not have been so great.

In contrast, analysis of the military cluster suggests the importance of continuing to assess evolving patterns in civil-military relations as these transitions move ahead. In both regions, one must be aware of the interpenetration of civilian and military roles inside and outside the state. This entails giving attention to the complex set of relationships involving military officers, enlisted men, and paramilitary groups outside the state, especially when there is a decision to act independently. Equally important is assessment of military bureaucrats: how they operate within the state apparatus and their corresponding links and ties with individuals and groups within the military institution and in civil society. While the outcomes differ greatly from country to country, these dynamics were very much a part of the Portuguese transition and are present in the Romanian, Bulgarian, and Yugoslav transitions. Furthermore, even though other military leaders, embracing a different combination of officers and enlisted men in Brazil and Chile, opted for very different strategies and produced yet another set of outcomes in South America, military actors have remained important ingredients in determing the course pursued in these transitions.

Hence, while the origins of the current economic and social crisis are very different in Latin America and Eastern Europe, there are important parallels in the social consequences of many of these transitions from authoritarian rule. If their economic and social outcomes are assessed comparatively and disaggregated according to country differences, the Portuguese case has far more to offer in those instances where there has been a marked rupture in the political, economic, and social structures identified with the prior regime.

Despite very different individual circumstances (viz, wartime conditions in Italy, successful prior economic reforms in Spain, and military disaster for Greece in Cyprus), all the Southern European transitions—except the Portuguese—took less time and focused much more on the negotiation of specific political accords among civilian elites. Similarly, in Poland, the Czech and Slovak Republics, and Hungary, the transitions to democratic rule were all accomplished quickly and decisively. There civilian oversight authority was quickly established and the military readily accepted the primacy that was to be given to civilian authorities in constituting successor regimes.

All the other countries embraced in the discussion here—fragmented societies with radically different concepts of state, society, and the economy among those competing for power—have had to pay a heavy price for prior decisions made in economic and social policy during the 1970s and 1980s. Each of them has had to face a major crisis of regime once the authority of the old regime was challenged from above and below. All have been burdened with the consequences of state-dominated economies, the shift from import-substitution to export-oriented economic growth strategies, centralized technocratic decision making, and hegemonic rule by political elites who have appropriated the instruments of governance to serve their own immediate ends. Such actions, taken prior to these transitions, have so constrained civil societies by consuming available economic and political resources that successor regimes have had little to no margin to attend to pressing economic and social needs. These are not abstract issues. Rather, they are tied up intimately with questions of governability and whether or not viable, lasting democratic regimes can be constructed under these conditions.

These same issues, choices, and policy constraints are all to be found in Portugal since 1974. The relevancy of the Portuguese transition and consolidation is that this occurred there earlier than has been the case in South America and the Balkans. Furthermore, despite considerable difficulties, the new military and civilian stakeholders who took command of politics and the economy in 1976 were able to confront these issues, to develop appropriate strategies for dealing with them, and to exercise conscious choices in reacting to the policy constraints facing them. But, while these stakeholders were successful in working out a new pattern of civil-military relations compatible with democracy, in dismantling the prior power structure centered around a strong state, and in consolidating a democratic political regime, they failed to engage suucessfully the issue of public sector reform.

Nevertheless, when it comes to questions of governance, the Portuguese response has been no different from that emerging later in in the Balkan and South American transitions.[3] In the rush to constitute markets and democracies, these countries' new leaders have all sidelined institutional questions. Yet, since institution building and development are tied to the capacity of these governments to design and implement programs and projects derived from policies designed to make markets and democracy work, these policy choices are likely to make consolidation more difficult. Because these states were originally patterned after Western experience and elites in these societies long have been imbued with self-images and life styles tied to European norms and values, policy makers have assumed that once their authoritarian legacies and preoccupation with questions of national security in the military and police were removed, these values and commitments would be sufficient to ensure success in these transitions. Yet, as can be seen from examining Portuguese experience in detail, this is not necessarily the case.

In the multinational and bilateral economic assistance offered to Portugal and states in Eastern Europe and the developed portions of South America, as well as in the response of host country governments to this assistance, it has been assumed that institution building initiatives are more appropriate in the structural adjustments and policy reforms required of lesser developed societies in Asia, Africa, and other parts of Latin America.[4] Much more common is a polemical literature in which the existing rhetoric and the ideological baggage inherited from the right and the left continue to impose blinders, with those identified with the previous regime pointing out the deterioration of economic and social conditions as a consequence of the excesses of freedom and those supporting the new order stressing the importance of the political accords reached and the procedures adopted to consolidate new regimes.

Commonalities Within Eastern Europe, South America, and Portugal

What are the commonalities between countries in Eastern Europe and Latin America which make comparison possible in the face of equally great disparities and differences between these two world regions? And, how does Portugal fit into this setting? While the first of these two questions has been deal with in two major publications on transitions, the second is the concern of this book.[5]

Certainly there is no doubt about the fact that we have behind us nearly half a century of world developments and intellectual traditions that speak to the uniqueness of each region—Marxist-Leninist ideology and Communist party rule in Eastern Europe, and dependent capitalism and the concentration of power in the hands of privileged minorities through the control of land, labor, and domestic capital, in Portugal and South America. To transcend these differences and comprehend the similarities of their current policy environment requires breaking the region down into sub-sets of states and keeping in mind several important distinctions within each region.

In Eastern Europe it is as important to separate the East-Central states of Poland, Hungary, and the former Czechoslovakia from the Balkan countries (the Yugoslav successor states, Romania, Bulgaria, and Albania), as it is to recognize that not all of Latin America is appropriate for such comparison. Democratic outcomes and conversion to market economies are far more likely to emerge eventually in East-Central Europe, where there is a prior history of economic and institutional development linking these areas to the European core. In contrast, in Southeastern Europe, the legacies of economic underdevelopment, authoritarianism, and xenophobic nationalism remain great. There redefinition of political communities and the elaboration of new and more appropriate state structures through which to govern various national groups are likely to consume far more time and greater energy, before attention can be turned to pressing economic and social issues and the consolidation of democratic regimes.

Likewise, the extent to which European points of reference are important in assessing the prospects for democracy and the development of productive market economies varies greatly within Latin America. Generally speaking, those Latin American cases which have evoked the greatest amount of Eastern European interest are the medium size and larger states on the South American continent. These are countries which have already consolidated state apparatuses in accord with Western models and have behind them significant experience in confronting issues of economic modernization, albeit with varying degrees of success. To date these cases largely comprise Brazil and Southern Cone South America—especially Argentina and Chile.[6]

In East-Central Europe and Southern Cone South America, democratic transitions and market liberalization are already well underway—at least in the sense of producing governments determined by regularly held open elections and economic policies linked to state shrinking and privatization, despite difficult economic and social conditions. In contrast, in Southeast Europe and in West Coast and Interior South America, democratic openings and movement away from state-dominated economies constitute much more tentative experiments. Hence, just as there is a cultural divide cutting across Eastern Europe, so too there is one cutting across South America. In the former, whether one was earlier subject to Austro-Hungarian or Ottoman Turkish rule still constitutes a valuable point of reference in the minds of their inhabitants in separating those areas whose experience has been essentially western from those considered to be outside Europe. Similarly, there is a division running across East Coast and West Coast South America, separating those areas where Iberian institutions and Southern European immigration have been dominant from those where westernization and assimilation of the local population into New World variants of Iberian culture have remained alien and far removed from local realities.[7]

If these differences are kept in mind, then they need to be matched with similar differentiations in Southern Europe. From this vantage point, while Spain and Portugal are usually paired in discussions of Western European politics, the differences between Spain and Portugal are enormous. Much more appropriate in these terms is the juxtaposition of Greece and Portugal, along with southern Italy, in confronting the problems and issues of state, society, and development policy. Portugal's political and economic evolution from the Napoleonic wars in the early 1800s down to 1974 placed it on the periphery of Europe far more than was the case with Spain. Throughout these years, and extending over more than a century, Portugal evolved in the direction of patterns of state and society much closer to those emergent in Brazil and the Southern Cone of South America.

Given these variations, the easiest place to begin in establishing a basis for comparison is by calling attention to the status of this particular group of countries historically as areas intimately tied up with the economic and political development of northwestern Europe and North America. Yet, at the very same time, they have remained at the margins of the modern industrial world. While the East-Central European countries, Brazil, the Southern Cone states, and Portugal were thoroughly integrated into the trading, commercial, and economic relations dominant before World War I and centered in northwestern Europe, the consequence of two world wars has been to marginalize both. Left in place in each case were national elites who had internalized what were largely European values regarding nation and state as well as economic modernization. Yet, in the new economic order which has been emerging since World War II, they have found themselves saddled with divided loyalties. On the one side stand their images of an older European world with which their ties have become increasingly tenuous, as a consequence of the disintegration of the Austro-Hungarian Empire, the declining weight of Great Britain as a world power, and the entrance into international affairs of radically different German, Japanese, and Soviet states during the interwar period and since World War II.

Matching profound changes at the international level are new national realities. As mass politics have emerged in all these societies, privileged groups—accustomed to limiting political participation and restricting access to power and the goods of society to a comfortable minority—have had to come to terms with new political forces who have sought to redefine state and nation in accord with their own particular domestic aspirations. While it was possible for these national elites to reaffirm their European ties and to either limit or control mass politics during the interwar period, increasingly both regions found themselves affected by economic nationalism and attracted to models of economic growth tied to national autarky. In Central Europe this was the consequence of the power vacuum left by the breakup of Austro-Hungary, whereas in the Southern Cone of South America this was due to the decline of the British imperial system.[8] For those who would argue that geographic proximity has always made the ties of the East-Central European states and Portugal with the West far closer than those of the Southern Cone, what reduced these differences and led to common perceptions of a shared semi-peripheral status were the outcomes of the Second World War, with the subjugation of Eastern Europe to Soviet control, the extension of U.S. hegemony over Latin America as a whole, and the inclusion of Portugal within the NATO alliance from its inception. Coupled with these developments was the relegation of these countries to secondary status as the superpowers accorded more attention to their own trans-Atlantic and trans-Pacific concerns and relationships.

Nevertheless, with the collapse of Soviet power in Eastern Europe in 1989 and growing economic challenges to U.S. influence in South America—first by Japan and the European Community and now by a united Germany, comparison of countries within the semi-periphery of Eastern and Southern Europe, along with the South American states, has become both possible and appropriate.

In each region prevailing political and economic formulas have been exhausted, without necessarily producing viable options and alternatives. While structural adjustment, policy reform, and privatization policies are shared in common today by these countries with many others around the world, it is the particular dynamic which has ensued in these regions that warrants attention apart. Into these discussions and considerations, it becomes essential to reintroduce questions related to civil-military relations and the viability of the state apparatus, since they constitute very different sets of interests in confronting issues related to regime consolidation.

As a consequence of past economic policy failures and current pressures (derived from structural adjustments required by international actors that cannot be implemented), this set of countries has fallen into a vicious cycle of continual policy reformulation because of the ineffectiveness of preceding policies. In each instance the social costs required exceed the tolerance of the very groups most needed for political support by elected presidents and representatives. National experiences in each region converge around a common litany of obstacles which continually undercut innovative policy agendas. Yet, it is this very convergence in policy that provides a basis for comparison. Each region contains state-dominated economies in which market mechanisms are weak and constrained. Each must devise without delay policies for producing more dynamic, growth-oriented markets and, in so doing, reduce the size of the public sector and redefine the role of the state. Each also is emerging from a prolonged era of authoritarian rule in which central planners and technocrats imposed economic and political policy through command and authority structures controlled by the state, with varying degrees of success and failure. In each the military institution, with its ties with the state and simultaneously with its interests outside the state and in civil society, constitutes a very different set of interests in national politics. With their previous authoritarian regimes now bankrupt and discredited, each is also faced with the challenge of consolidating democratic regimes in which the partisans of authoritarian rule—be they on the right or the left—must be kept marginalized and rendered ineffective, if these new endeavors are to be successful.

Toward a New Basis for Comparison

If this broader picture is considered, the challenge is to devise a more holistic frame of reference, capable of integrating political, economic, and managerial perspectives in such a way as to pinpoint a common set of policy issues. Also needed is comparative data on parallel experiences in such areas as trade liberalization, public enterprise performance, privatization, and labor and wage policy. Equally important is the attempt to clarify more effectively the choices at stake, in the specific policies and programs which must follow in order to achieve that economic restructuring necessary for the consolidation of competitive markets throughout East-Central Europe, Portugal, Brazil, and the Southern Cone.

If such a vantage point is adopted, there are four crucial areas of common concern in which comparative research carries with it the potential for greater policy relevance.

First, within East-Central Europe (Poland, the Czech and Slovak Republics, Hungary) as within Portugal, Brazil, and the Southern Cone (Argentina, Uruguay, Chile), state-centered economic development was linked in the past with substantial, initial success in the transformation of these societies. In both instances, however, as these economies matured, it became apparent that the long-term results were mixed. Governments found it enormously difficult to transcend the limitations of this economic model (with its emphasis on state-controlled economies) and the constraints imposed by prior structural decisions. While all eight countries made major advances during the 1950s and the early 1960s, by the late 1960s economic constraints and structural problems had become more and more apparent.

In Brazil and the Southern Cone, inflation combined with the exhaustion of import-substitution industrialization presented policy makers with a very difficult set of choices. The authoritarian regimes dominant in the late 1960s and the early 1970s all experimented with innovative technocratic economic reforms that gave the illusion of significant change. But, whatever the success claimed, what must never be forgotten is that these economic policies were pursued in the context of repressive regimes that demonstrated flagrant disregard for individual human rights.

While various reformist packages have been attempted since, none has been able to resolve the basic problem that fundamental economic restructuring requires enormous social costs. In the present context of fragile new democratic regimes, it remains to be seen if elected governments will have the capacity politically to sustain the changes needed. In Eastern Europe, the emphasis on mass industrialization under centrally-planned economies began to run into more and more difficulties in the late 1960s, for which there was pressure for economic and political reform. While the dates vary considerably in Argentina, Chile, and Brazil, in both regions there is a parallel cycle of extensive state expansion linked with the drive to establish mass industries. The consequence of these policies was incomplete transformation of the economy, so that when the drive began a decade later to produce more competitive export commodities, the low quality of the commercial and industrial goods produced made them largely non-competitive in world markets. A flurry of extensive borrowing abroad ensued and these countries attracted international credits in varying amounts during the early 1970s. While this infusion of external economic resources seemed to offset earlier problems and led to excessive optimism and enhanced expectations regarding a new breakthrough in economic growth, the result by the late 1970s and early 1980s was the return of inflationary pressures coupled now with severe economic constraints on further borrowing, with no easy recourse to new economic credits and loans abroad.

Again, while the experience with the responses to these crises vary greatly (with a certain degree of success being achieved in market reforms in Chile and Hungary as opposed to sustained economic crisis in Argentina and Poland during the 1980s), the issues being grappled with in all of them now concern how to reduce further the state's role in the economy, as well as how to accomplish trade liberalization, privatization of public enterprises, and the revival of market economies. While these issues are proving difficult to resolve in East-Central Europe, they are even more problematic in the Balkans.

Second, in the process of stimulating economic development through state initiatives and state control of the economy, in each of these regions the development of the middle sectors of society produced a new class of party politicians, more highly trained bureaucrats with advanced education in economics, engineering, and planning, and new professionalism in the armed forces and the paramilitary police organizations associated with them. While these phenomena differ considerably in the distinct economic bases of the two orders—mixed market economies in South America and centrally planned, command economies in Easern Europe—both patterns of state-centered economic growth have produced a new class of state functionaries and clienteles dependent on the state for their employment and largess. In Eastern Europe this is the nomenklatura, to which Milovan Djilas attached the label "the new class." In Portugal, Brazil and the Southern Cone, one can identify three closely related sectors that have produced the same consequences: a new class of professional military officers identified with a national security ethos; professional politicians (astute individuals, usually trained in the law who have developed careers centered around politics, parties, and legislatures); and public functionaries (*funcionários públicos*) dependent on government for their economic survival. In this regard, if we are indebted to Djilas for the concept of the new class, it is Hélio Jaguaribe and his coining of the phrase "the cartorial state" (*o estado cartorial*)—the bureaucratic, legalistic state with its extensive dependent clienteles—that best gives expression to this phenomen in Portugal and South America.[9]

Third, following regime crises that brought down bureaucratic-authoritarian states on the right as well as on the left, the East-Central and Southeastern European states and the East Coast and West Coast South American states have all been engaged in transition politics. This has been accompanied by a search for effective economic reforms which will move these countries away from state-centered development initiatives toward free-market economies. In politics, this has been matched by the search for policies that will move these regimes from transitional democracies into consolidated democracies—where, despite the outcomes, all power contenders will seek to resolve their differences through elections and competition to determine the design and content of public policies.

Again, despite the differences between the two processes—the abandonment of military-dominated governments in Portugal and South America and the collapse of Communist regimes in Eastern Europe—there are marked similarities in the convergence of economic and political factors in these two regions. These convergences point to the realization that there are no easy solutions to the problems at hand and that these transitions are certain to be prolonged. While the process has only just begin in Eastern Europe, the complexity of the issues confronted by these countries suggests that the process of economic and political transformation is more likely to parallel Portuguese and South American experience, rather than that of either Italy or Spain.

Consider the record to date. In Portugal, the transition has taken 15 years (1974-1989). There one can speak of democratic consolidation only since the last round of constitutional changes, executed in 1989. In Brazil, the transition took a decade of negotiations before there was concurrence on permitting a civilian to take command of the presidency (1974-1985).

And now, after seven years of civilian rule since the changeover, one still cannot speak of successful democratic consolidation. Furthermore, if one considers the disintegration of state structures in Peru and Bolivia and compares these patterns with those underway in Yugoslavia and Albania, there is a growing discrepancy in all four between state apparatuses, long used as instruments of domination with a waning capacity to impose policy by fiat, and national communities reorganizing and mobilizing themselves from below and outside the state.

Fourth, the economic prescriptions spelled out for restructuring these economies and moving them toward more dynamic markets are strikingly similar. To cite but a few of the economic management capacities stressed as essential for these eight countries by international actors, there is remarkable consistency in the following list, each of which assumes the prior existence of a coherent state apparatus to achieve success:

more effective public sector management; privatization and industrial restructuring; the development of a more appropriate financial environment (i.e., more effective institutions and systems for banking, capital markets, and tax administration coupled with training in the skills of asset valuation, accounting, and commercial banking practices); the provision of a more adequate social safety net; the reversal of poor agriculture productivity; improvements in the telecommunications network; the restructuring of the transport sector; attention to the massive pollution of the environment; and enhancement of the nation's productive technology, in terms of giving attention to developing policies, strategies, and programs for research and development in all key sectors of the economy.

It is precisely the similarities encountered in the above check list, developed from the requirements common to so many structural adjustment programs, and the very different ways in which individual governments in these countries are responding to them, that provides such a challenge.

One place where we might well begin in new, more policy-relevant social science research is by identifying more clearly the commonalities present in specific parts of Eastern Europe, Southern Europe, and South

America, where it is clear that economic and political restructuring are essential to the development of market economies and the consolidation of democratic regimes. The policy choices pursued and the successes and failures encountered already in these countries provide a range of variation in policy performance that offers new and creative insight into what are obviously very difficult and simultaneously very important policy issues. Such matters are not merely academic in nature and import. They have enormous policy relevance in the new world that is emerging in which few of the prescriptions of the past will be sufficient to carry us ahead into a world that is more interrelated and interdependent than ever before.

However, before progress can be made in these areas through more rigorous comparative analysis, it is essential to block in individual country case experience. For, while these patterns in economic modernization are similar across the cases brought into this discussion, the individuality of each superimposes a range of contrasting experiences that cannot be overlooked. The intent, then, in this particular analysis of Portuguese experience has been to develop a theoretically relevant case study that can open up comparative work on the transition to and consolidation of democratic regimes and market economies to new vistas.

The extended attention given to civil-military relations, however, should not lead to the conclusion that the military is and will always be central in such transitions. Rather, it is designed to call attention to the fact that in the Portuguese case the break with the past and the need to restructure politics, society, and the economy radically, in the aftermath of authoritarian rule, required the development of a new dynamic between civilian and military actors. And, that one of the consequences of the settlement reached among these actors was a weak state, continually bypassed and superseded by initiatives outside the state during the 1980s. The weakness of Portugal's state apparatus increasingly has placed the government in a situation where during the 1990s economic progress of benefit to a minority at the expense of the majority appears to have been purchased at the expense of national sovereignty.

In each of these cases, what I have termed "the military cluster of interests" requires separate analysis and consideration. In weighing the prospects for democratic consolidation, this cluster must be disaggregated into key individuals and groups and evaluated according to how they will react to political, economic, and social issues. This is especially necessary when civilian leaders wish to carry out policies that lead the country in directions military leaders define as against their institutional interests.

The other side of this equation is the problem of the state apparatus and the importance of giving serious consideration to the kind of state desired over the short, medium, and long term, in moving from a transitional to a consolidated democracy. By disaggregating world regions traditionally dealt with as containing distinct bodies of experience, attention here has centered on structural similarities among a particular group of countries that cut across Eastern and Southern Europe and across East Coast and West Coast South America. In them, both the military and the state figure in as important independent variables affecting directly the prospects for the consolidation of democracies and market economies.

Notes

1. The one instance of major public sector reform is Chile, but there the reforms are linked to economic policy choices made by the Pinochet government in the early 1980s, well in advance of the transition back to democracy.

2. While the works of Immanuel Wallerstein, especially *The Modern World System* (New York: Academic Press, 1974), have been seminal in current concepts of center and periphery in the economic and political development of the modern world, the more specific concept often used for these cases is that of "the semi-periphery." For this application of Wallerstein's original ideas to Southern Europe and South America, see: Allan Williams (ed.), *Southern Europe Transformed: Political and Economic Change in Greece, Italy, Portugal, and Spain* (London: Harper and Row, 1984); Nicos Mouzelis, *Politics in the Semi-Periphery: Early Parliamentarism and Late Industrialization in the Balkans and Latin America* (New York: St. Martin's Press, 1986); and Kathleen C. Schwartzman, *The Social Origins of Democratic Collapse: The First Portuguese Republic in the Global Economy* (Lawrence: University Press of Kansas, 1989]).

3. For a discussion of this dimension in South America, see Alfred Stephan, "State Power and the Strength of Civil Society in the Southern Cone of South America," in Peter B. Evans, Dietrich Rueschemeyer, and Theda Skocpol (eds.), *Bringing the State Back In*, (New York: Cambridge University Press, 1985), pp. 317-43.

4. Portugal is a case in point. Whereas an extended time line is not available for examining the consequence of structural adjustment and policy reform initiatives in Eastern Europe and South America, there is more than a decade of extended assistance to Portugal at the time its leaders were engaged in the politics of transition. While Eanes did attempt at one point to initiate public administration reforms, which would have increased the capacity of the Portuguese state to implement policy, partisan politics and the policy preferences of party leaders in the National Assembly made this impossible. Documentation of the economic thrust of foreign assistance and the exclusion of institution building initiatives, on the grounds that Portugal was a Western European country and that experience acquired in the non-European world was irrelevant, can be found in the following report: F. F. Simmons, L. S. Graham and J. J. Buttari, "Portugal: Program and Management Impact Evaluation" (Agency for International Development) (Washington, DC: Development Associates, 1983).

5. The first scholar to engage this issue was Adam Przeworski in "The 'East' Becomes the 'South'? The 'Autumn of the People' and the Future of Eastern Europe," in PS: Political Science and Politics, 24:1 (March 1991), pp. 20-24, and *Democracy and the Market: Political and Economic Reforms in Eastern Europe and Latin America* (New York: Cambridge University Press, 1991). A more in-depth treatment of the topic, including further development of the concept of transition games by Prezorwski, is to be found in Scott Mainwaring, Guillermo O'Donnel, and J. Samuel Valenzuela (eds.), *Issues in Democratic Consolidation: The New South American Democracies in Comparative Perspective* (Notre Dame, IN: Notre Dame University Press, 1992).

6. The book which most successfully captures this interest is one edited by the Polish economic historian, Henryk Szlajfer, *Economic Nationalism in East-Central Europe and South America, 1918-1939* (Geneva: Centre of International Economic History, University of Geneva, 1990).

7. For those who would define all of Brazil as Southern Cone, it is appropriate to return to a Brazilian classic in the confrontation between a coastal culture and civilization that was European in its derivation and a distinct world in the interior of the northeast in which the local population was an amalgam of Indian, African, and colonial Portuguese peoples and assimilated into a set of experiences which were essentially non-western: Euclides da Cunha, *Rebellion in the Backlands (Os Sertões)* Chicago: University of Chicago Press, 1944). For yet another literary account of a non-western world in South America, see Ciro Alegria's classic about the peoples of highland Peru, *Broad and Alien Is the World (El Mundo Es Ancho y Ajeno)* (New York: Farrar and Rinehart, 1941).

8. The primary sources utilizing a comparative approach in the analysis of the interwar economic history of these two regions are Henryk Szlajfer's *Economic Nationalism in East-Central Europe and South America, 1918-1939* and Nicos P. Mouzelis, *Politics in the Semi-Periphery: Early Parliamentarism and Late Industrialization in the Balkans and Latin America.*

9. The publications where these ideas are most clearly stated are: Milovan Djilas, *The New Class: An Analysis of the Communist System* (New York: Praeger Publishers, 1957) and Hélio Jaguaribe, *Condições Institucionais do Desenvolvimento* (Rio de Janeiro: Ministério de Educação e Cultura, Instituto Superior de Estudos Brasileiros, 1958).

References

Alegria, Ciro. 1941. *Broad and Alien Is the World (El Mundo Es Ancho y Ajeno)*. New York: Farrar and Rinehart.

Almeida Fernandes, Miguel. 1981. "A reestruturação nas Forças Armadas: Estudo de psicólogos indica Melo Egídio como o homem certo para CEMGFA," *Expresso*, (21 February): 3.

"Armed Forces: 'Silent Majority' Commands." 1981. Special supplement on Portugal, *International Herald Tribune*, (3 June): 14S.

Azeredo, Carlos de. 1984. *As populações a norte do Douro e os franceses em 1808 e 1809*. Porto: Museu Militar do Porto.

Barany, Zoltan. 1993. "Regional Disparities and Civil-Military Relations: East-Central and Southeastern Europe," in Lawrence S. Graham, ed., "Political and Economic Transitions in Eastern Europe and Latin America" (unpublished book manuscript).

Barreto, António Barreto. 1984. "Estado central e descentralização: antecedentes e evolução, 1974-84," *Análise Social*, 20: 191—217.

Braga da Cruz, Manuel. 1986. "A Evolução das Instituições Políticas: Partidos Políticos e Forças Armadas na Transição Democrática Portuguesa (1974-1986)," *Povos e Culturas*, No. 1: 205—15.

Bruneau, Thomas C. 1983. "Popular Support for Democracy in Post-Revolutionary Portugal: Results from a Survey," in Lawrence S. Graham and Douglas L. Wheeler, eds., *In Search of Modern Portugal: The Revolution and Its Consequences*. Madison: University of Wisconsin Press.

—. 1984. *Politics and Nationhood: Post-Revolutionary Portugal*. New York: Praeger Publishers.

— and Alex Macleod. 1986. *Politics in Contemporary Portugal: Parties and the Consolidation of Democracy.* Boulder, CO: Lynne Rienner Publishers.

Burton, Michael G., and John Higley. 1987. "Elite Settlements," in *Texas Papers on Latin America,* No. 87-01. Austin: Institute of Latin American Studies, University of Texas at Austin.

Carrilho, Maria. 1985. *Forças Armadas e Mudança Política em Portugal no Sec. XX: Para uma explicação sociólogica do papel dos militares.* Lisbon: Estudos Gerais, Série Universitária, Imprensa Nacional—Casa da Moeda.

Coelho, Mario Baptista, ed. 1989. *Portugal: O Sistema Político e Constitucional, 1974-1987.* Lisbon: Instituto de Ciências Sociais.

Costa Pinto, António. 1991. "The Salazar 'New State' and European Fascism," *EUI Working Paper HEC,* No. 91/12. Badia Fiesolana, San Domenico, Italy: European University Institute.

Cunha, Euclides da. 1944. *Rebellion in the Backlands (Os Sertões).* Chicago: University of Chicago Press.

Deák, István. 1992. "Survivors," *The New York Review of Books,* (5 March): 43—51.

Defense and Foreign Affairs Handbook. 1986. Washington, DC: Perth Corp.

Diamond, Larry, Juan J. Linz, and Seymour Martin Lipset, eds. 1989. *Democracy in Developing Countries: Latin America,* vol. 4. Boulder, CO: Lynne Rienner Publishers.

Djilas, Milovan. 1957. *The New Class: An Analysis of the Communist System.* New York: Praeger Publishers.

Evans, Peter, Dietrich Rueschemeyer, and Theda Skocpol, eds. 1985. *Bringing the State Back In.* Princeton, NJ: Princeton University Press.

Expresso (Lisbon, Portugal, weekly newspaper: random issues).

Faoro, Raymundo. 1975. *Os Donos do Poder: Formação do Patronato Político Brasileiro.* Porto Alegre: Editora Globo (2d rev. ed. 2 vols.).

"A Formação de Portugal Contemporâneo, 1900-1980." 1982 and 1983. Vols. 1—2. *Análise Social*, 18: Nos. 72—74 and 19: Nos. 77-79 (special issue: symposium vols.).

Freitas do Amaral, Diogo. 1983. *A Lei de Defesa Nacional e das Forças Armadas (Textos, discursos e trabalho preparatórios)*. Coimbra: Coimbra Editora.

—. 1987. "A Elaboração da Lei de Defesa Nacional e das Forças Armadas," in *A Feitura das Leis*, vol. 1 (Oeiras: no publisher). Pp. 117—38.

—. 1989. "A Constituição e as Forças Armadas," in Mário Baptista Coelho, ed., *Portugal: O Sistema Político e Constitucional, 1974-1987*. Lisbon: Instituto de Ciências Sociais.

Graham, Lawrence S. 1975. *Portugal: The Decline and Collapse of an Authoritarian Order*. Beverly Hills, CA: Sage Professional Papers in Comparative Politics, vol. 1, no. 01—001, Sage Publications.

—. 1979. "The Military in Politics: The Politicization of the Portuguese Armed Forces," in Lawrence S. Graham and Harry M. Makler, eds., *Contemporary Portugal: The Revolution and Its Antecedents*. Austin: University of Texas Press.

—. 1979. "Is the Portuguese Revolution Dead?." *Luso-Brazilian Review*, 16: 2 (Winter).

—. 1983. "Bureaucratic Politics and the Problem of Reform in the State Apparatus," in Lawrence S. Graham and Douglas L. Wheeler, eds., *In Search of Modern Portugal: The Revolution and Its Consequences*. Madison: University of Wisconsin Press.

—. 1990. "Center-Periphery Relations," in Kenneth Maxwell and Michael H. Haltzel, eds., *Portugal: Ancient Country, Young Democracy*. Washington, DC: The Wilson Center Press.

—. 1990. *The State and Policy Outcomes in Latin America*, especially chapter 8. New York: Praeger (Hoover Institution Series).

—. 1991. "Institutionalizing Democracy: Governance in Post-1974 Portugal," in Ali Farazmand, ed., *Handbook of Comparative and Development Public Administration*. New York: Marcel Dekker.

—. 1991. "Redefining the Portuguese Transition to Democracy," in John Higley and Richard Gunther, eds., *Elites and Democratic Consolidation in Latin America and Southern Europe*. New York: Cambridge University Press.

Hammond, John L. 1988. *Building Popular Power: Workers' and Neighborhood Movements in the Portuguese Revolution*. New York: Monthly Review Press.

Huntington, Samuel P. 1957. *The Soldier and the State: The Theory and Politics of Civil-Military Relations*. Cambridge: Harvard University Press.

Jaguaribe, Hélio. 1958. *Condições Institucionais do Desenvolvimento*. Rio de Janeiro: Ministério de Educação e Cultura, Instituto Superior de Estudos Brasileiros.

Kramer, Jane. 1992. "Letter from Europe (Otelo Nuno Romano Saraiva de Carvalho and the Portuguese Revolution)," *The New Yorker*, 63 (30 November): 105 ff.

LaFranchi, Howard. 1992. "Greece, Portugal Test EC Capacity to Grow," *Christian Science Monitor* (23 July): 6—7.

Leeds, Elizabeth. 1984. "Labor Export, Development, and the State: The Political Economy of Portuguese Emigration" (unpublished doctoral dissertation). Cambridge, MA: Massachusetts Institute of Technology.

Mainwaring, Scott, Guillermo O'Donnell, and J. Samuel Valenzuela, eds., 1992. *Issues in Democratic Consolidation: The New South American Democracies in Comparative Perspective*. Notre Dame, IN: University of Notre Dame Press.

Maxwell, Kenneth. 1986. "Regime Overthrow and the Prospects for Democratic Transition in Portugal," in Guillermo O'Donnell, Philippe C. Schmitter, and Laurence Whitehead, eds., *Transitions from Authoritarian Rule: Southern Europe*. Baltimore: Johns Hopkins University Press.

—, ed. 1991. *Portuguese Defense and Foreign Policy Since Democratization*. Camões Center Special Report No. 3. New York: Research Institute on International Change, Columbia University.

—. 1991. "Spain's Transition to Democracy: A Model for Eastern Europe?" in Nils H. Wessell, ed., *The New Europe: Revolution in East-West Relations*. New York: The Academy of Political Science.

Medeiros Ferreira, José. 1989. "Um corpo perante o Estado: militares e instituições políticas," in Mário Baptista Coelho, ed., *Portugal: O Sistema Político e Constitucional, 1974-1987.* Lisbon: Instituto de Ciências Sociais.

Migdal, Joel S. 1988. *Strong Societies and Weak States: State-Society Relations and State Capabilities in the Third World.* Princeton, NJ: Princeton University Press.

Mouzelis, Nicos. 1986. *Politics in the Semi-Periphery: Early Parliamentarism and Late Industrialization in the Balkans and Latin America.* New York: St. Martin's Press.

"Mudanças Sociais no Portugal de Hoje: Comunicações ao Colóquio Organizado pelo Instituto de Ciências Sociais." 1985. *Análise Social*, 21: Nos. 87—89 (special issue: symposium papers).

Nelson, Joan M., ed. 1990. *Economic Crisis and Policy Choice: The Politics of Adjustment in the Third World.* Princeton, NJ: Princeton University Press.

North Atlantic Treaty Organization: Facts and Figures. 1981. Brussels: NATO Information Service.

O'Donnell, Guillermo, Philippe C. Schmitter, and Laurence Whitehead, eds. 1986. *Transitions from Authoritarian Rule: Prospects for Democracy.* Baltimore, MD: The Johns Hopkins University Press.

Opello, Walter. 1985. *Portugal's Political Development: A Comparative Approach.* Boulder, CO: Westview Press.

Porch, Douglas. 1977. *The Portuguese Armed Forces and Revolution.* Stanford, CA: Hoover Institution Press.

Portugal, Ministério da Defesa Nacional. 1986. *Livro Branco da Defesa Nacional.* Lisbon: Gabinete do Ministro, Ministério da Defesa Nacional.

"Portugal Survey." 1988. *The Economist* (28 May) (supplement).

Przeworski, Adam. 1991. *Democracy and the Market: Political and Economic Reforms in Eastern Europe and Latin America.* New York: Cambridge University Press.

—. "The 'East" Becomes the 'South'? The 'Autumn of the People' and the Future of Eastern Europe." 1991. *PS: Political Science and Politics*, 24: 20—24.

Raby, David L. 1983. "Populism and the Portuguese Left: From Delgado to Otelo," in Lawrence S. Graham and Douglas L. Wheeler, eds., *In Search of Modern Portugal: The Revolution and Its Consequences*. Madison: The University of Wisconsin Press.

Ramet, Sabrina Petra. "The Serbian Church and the Serbian Nation." 1992. Unpublished paper presented at the panel on "Religion in Eastern Europe in the Post-Communist Era." Phoenix, AZ: National Convention of the American Association for the Advancement of Slavic Studies (19-22 November).

Rouquié, Alain. 1987. *The Military and the State in Latin America*, trans. Paul E. Sigmund. Berkeley and Los Angeles: University of California Press.

"Salgado Zenha: O Governo sofre do optimismo panglóssico do dr. Soares" (interview). 1987. *Expresso*, magazine supplement (14 February): 35R.

Schmitter, Philippe C. 1979. "The 'Regime d'Exception' That Became the Rule: Forty-Eight Years of Authoritarian Domination in Portugal," in Lawrence S. Graham and Harry M. Makler, eds., *Contemporary Portugal: The Revolution and Its Antecedents*. Austin: University of Texas Press.

Schwartzman, Kathleen C. 1989. *The Social Origins of Democratic Collapse: The First Portuguese Republic in the Global Economy*. Lawrence: University Press of Kansas.

"Shrinking Power: Network of U.S. Bases Overseas Is Unraveling As Need for It Grows." 1987. *Wall Street Journal (WSJ)*, (29 December): 5.

Simmons, F. F., L. S. Graham and J. J. Buttari. 1983. "Portugal: Program and Management Impact Evaluation" (Agency for International Development). Washington, DC: Development Associates.

Smith, Diana. 1990. *Portugal and the Challenge of 1992*. Camões Center Special Report No. 1. New York: Research Institute on International Change, Columbia University.

Solano, C. B., J. L. Barros Horcasitas, and J. Hurtado, eds. 1991. *Transiciones a la Democracia en Europa y América Latina*. Mexico: Facultad Latinoamericana de Ciencias Sociales y Universidad de Guadalajara.

Sousa Ferreira, Eduardo, and Walter C. Opello, Jr., eds. 1985. *Conflictos e Mudanças em Portugal, 1974-1984*. Lisboa: Teorema.

Sousa Santos, Boaventura de. 1984. "A Crise e a Reconstituição do Estado em Portugal (1974-84)," *Revista Crítica de Ciências Sociais*, No. 14: 7—29.

—. 1990. *O Estado e a Sociedade em Portugal (1974-1988)*. Porto: Edições Afrontamento.

Sparrow, Bartholomew H. 1991. "Review Essay: The State and the Politics of Oil," *Theory and Society*, 20: 259—81.

—. "Skocpol and the American State" (unpublished paper). 1990. San Francisco, CA: Annual Meeting of the American Political Science Association.

Stepan, Alfred. 1988. *Rethinking Military Politics: Brazil and the Southern Cone*. Princeton, NJ: Princeton University Press.

Szlajfer, Henryk, ed. 1990. *Economic Nationalism in East-Central Europe and South America, 1918-1939*. Geneva: Centre of International Economic History, University of Geneva.

U.S. Department of State, Bureau of Public Affairs, Office of Public Communication. 1987. *Background Notes: Portugal* (November). Washington, DC: U.S. Department of State.

Weekly Compilation of Presidential Documents. 1988. Monday 29 February, Vol. 24, No. 8: 251. Washington, DC.

Wallerstein, Immanuel. 1974. *The Modern World System*. New York: Academic Press.

Wheeler, Douglas. 1979. "The Military and the Portuguese Dictatorship, 1926-1974: 'The Honor of the Army,'" in Lawrence S. Graham and Harry M. Makler, eds., *Contemporary Portugal: The Revolution and Its Antecedents*. Austin: University of Texas Press.

—. 1986. *A Ditadura Militar Portuguesa, 1926-1933*. Mém Martins, Portugal: Publicações Europa-América.

Wiarda, Howard. 1989. *The Transition to Democracy in Spain and Portugal*. Lanham, MD: American Enterprise Institute for Public Policy Research.

Williams, Allan, ed. 1984. *Southern Europe Transformed: Political and Economic Change in Greece, Italy, Portugal, and Spain*. London: Harper and Row.

World Development Report 1991: The Challenge of Development. 1991. New York: World Bank, Oxford University Press.

Zaverucha, Jorge. 1992. "Degree of Military Political Autonomy During the Spanish, Argentine, and Brazilian Transitions." Unpublished conference paper. Los Angeles, CA: Latin American Studies Association XVII International Congress (24-27 September).

—. 1993. "The 1988 Brazilian Constitution or How to Harm Civilian Control over the Military," in Lawrence S. Graham, ed., "Political and Economic Transitions in Eastern Europe and Latin America" (unpublished book manuscript).

Index

Africa
  North Africa, 93
  Portuguese colonies in, 15-20,
    94, 97
  Portuguese military in, 18,
    19-21, 39-40, 65
  Spínola's plan for, 19
Agricultural cooperatives, 25
  Air force, 41, 44, 47, 54, 64. *See
    also* Military
Albania, 122, 129
Alves, Lopes, 33
Angola, 15, 18, 19, 38, 39, 94
Aparício, José, 33
April 25th Association, 53, 55
April 25 Movement. *See* Movement
    of the 25th of April
    (Movimento 25 de Abril)
Argentina, 1, 5, 117, 122, 126, 127
Armed forces. *See* Military
Armed Forces Assembly, 24-25,
    83-84
Armed Forces Movement. *See* MFA
    (Armed Forces Movement)
Army. *See* Military
Arriaga, Kaúlza de, 19
Assembly of the Armed Forces
    Movement. *See* Armed
    Forces Assembly
Assembly of the Republic, 13, 14,
    32, 42, 44, 45, 48, 49, 51, 52,
    66, 71, 74, 83, 85-87, 92, 99,
    103

Austro-Hungary, 122, 123, 124
Authoritarian regimes, breakdown
    of, 1-8
Azores, 52, 67, 95

Balkans, 2, 5, 66, 75, 116-118,
    120-122, 127
Balsemão, Francisco, 51, 54
Bloco Central (Central Bloc), 51
Bolivia, 129
Brazil, 3, 4, 7, 37-38, 117, 119, 122,
    123, 126-129, 133(n7)
Bruneau, Thomas C., 45
Bulgaria, 119

Cabinets (Governos), 45, 48, 49, 50
Cabora Bassa dam project, 18
Caetano, Marcello, 15-22, 35(n9),
    39, 40, 43, 70, 93, 94, 96, 97
Captains' Movement, 19
Cartorial state, 128
Carvalho, Otelo Saraiva de. *See*
    Otelo Saraiva de Carvalho
Cavaco Silva, Aníbal, 51, 52,
    62(n16), 67
CDS. *See* Social Democratic Center
    (CDS)
Ceausescu regime, 118
Central Bloc (Bloco Central), 51
Charais, Lt. Colonel Manuel
    Franco, 28
Checks and balances, 14

144

transition to democracy in, 5,
10-34, 128
unresolved issues in
civil-military relations, 67-68
Portuguese Communist Party
(PCP), 17, 20, 26, 29, 31, 32,
85, 87, 90(n7)
Portuguese General Staff
(EMGFA), 18, 24, 31, 32,
42-44, 47, 49, 50, 52, 66, 68,
71-74, 86
Portuguese Socialist Party (PS), 28,
32, 46, 49, 51, 85, 87, 90(n7),
98
Postal service, 112
PRD, 51, 52, 90(n7)
Presidency. *See also* names of
specific presidents
as commander-in-chief of
armed forces, 47, 49, 50, 71,
73
in Constitution, 13, 14, 42, 92
Eanes's strengthening of, 32, 44
relationship with prime
minister, 50, 52, 54, 72-73,
86, 103
Presidency of the Council of
Ministers, 70, 72, 96
Prime minister
changes in role of, 92
as civilian appointment, 32
in Constitution, 13, 14, 42
Eanes's view of, 31
and national defense, 48, 49, 50,
52
relationship with president, 50,
52, 54, 72-73, 86, 103
Privatization, 87, 117
PRP-BR (Partido Revolucionário
do Proletariado-Brigadas
Revolucionárias), 27

PS. *See* Portuguese Socialist Party
(PS)
PSD. *See* Social Democratic Party
(PSD)
PSP. *See* Policia de Segurança
Pública (PSP)
Public employment, 94-95, 97-99,
107-108, 114(n6), 115(n9),
127-128
Public health services, 101-102,
109-112
Public services, 101-102, 109-112
Public transportation, 111
Public Works Ministry, 114(n5)

Reagan, Ronald, 62(n16)
Regime, definition of, 79(n7)
Retornados, 26
Revolution of 1974, 6, 21-25, 81, 93,
95, 104, 118
Revolution of Flowers, 40
Revolutionary council. *See* Council
of the Revolution
Rocha Vieira, General Vasco, 43, 52
Romania, xi, xii(n2), 118, 119, 122
Rosa Coutinho, Vice Admiral
António Alva, 23, 26, 27
Rural areas, and Revolution of
1974, 25

Sá Carneiro, Francisco, 14, 32, 45,
51, 85
Salazar, António, 14-17, 35(n9), 39,
40, 69, 70, 96, 97, 104,
114(n5)
Salgado Zenha, Francisco, 52
Saneamento (cleansing), 97-98
Saraiva de Carvalho, Otelo. *See*
Otelo Saraiva de Carvalho
Schmitter, Philippe, 7

Transportation, 111
Trindade, Gen. Aurélio, 50
Turkey, 1, 93

Union of Soviet Socialist Republics.
    See Soviet Union
UNITA, 38
United Kingdom, 13
United States
    civil-military relations in, 46,
        61(n8)
    and Latin America, 124
    military assistance to Portugal,

55-56, 58-59, 66
Uruguay, 7, 126
U.S.S.R. *See* Soviet Union

Varela Gomes, Colonel João, 26, 27

Water service, 111
Whitehead, Laurence, 7

Yugoslavia, 4, 6, 119, 122, 129

Zaire, 18